A HISTORY OF
THE ATKINSON MORLEY'S
1869–1995

A HISTORY OF
THE ATKINSON
MORLEY'S HOSPITAL

1869–1995

TERRY GOULD & DAVID UTTLEY

ATHLONE
London & Atlantic Highlands

First published 1996 by
THE ATHLONE PRESS LTD
1 Park Drive, London NW11 7SG
and 165 First Avenue,
Atlantic Highlands, NJ 07716

British Library Cataloguing in Publication Data
*A catalogue record for this book is available
from the British Library*

ISBN 0 485 11505 0 hb
0 485 12125 5 pb

Library of Congress Cataloging-in-Publication Data
Gould, Terry, 1931–
    A history of Atkinson Morley's Hospital, 1869–1995 / by
Terry Gould and David Uttley.
        p.   cm.
    Includes bibliographical references and index.
    ISBN 0-485-11505-0 (cloth). - ISBN 0 485-12125-5 (pbk.)
    1. Atkinson Morley's Hospital.   2. Nervous system--Dis-
eases--Hospitals--England--London--History.   3. Wimbledon (London, England)   I. Uttley, David.   II. Title.
RC328.G68   1996
362.1′1′0942193--dc20   96-21899
                                                                  CIP

Typeset by
Bibloset

Printed and bound in Great Britain by
the University Press, Cambridge

Contents

PROLOGUE

Acknowledgements

We would like to thank John Fisher, for his invaluable help and the Guildhall Library, Corporation of London for kind permission to reproduce the engraving of Morley's Hotel.

We are also, grateful to Mrs Margot Curran, Mrs Joyce Williams and Dr Ivan Mosely for their help in rectifying deficiencies in the Archives Department of St.George's Hospital.

Introduction

The Atkinson Morley's Hospital has stood proudly on the south side of Copse Hill in Wimbledon for over one hundred and twenty five years. Indeed from the northbound A3 at Raynes Park it very much resembles a French Chateau perched on the skyline, this is not surprising as it was greatly influenced by the architectural ideals of the Second Empire. It was built as a convalescent hospital: the very first purpose built sanatorium to be associated with an inner city hospital. It had a major change of use during World War II and became over the years what it now is: an internationally recognised Neuroscience Centre. Because of its unusual name and the great esteem in which it is held, a keen interest in the hospital's origin and its subsequent development has been kindled in many of the patients who have been treated at the hospital, and members of staff who have worked there. Katherine Garton, a former librarian of the hospital wrote an excellent monograph about the hospital in the 1970s but sadly her book has been out of print for some years so, with a major anniversary just completed, it seemed a suitable time to attempt a further version. We are indebted to the countless anonymous members of staff of St. George's and the Atkinson Morley's Hospitals who kept such full and accurate records over the years which greatly simplified the writing of this book; and we gratefully acknowledge the help that Andrew Rolland, Kate Hayward and Debbie Lock have given us, but the writers must shoulder the blame for any omission or inaccuracy. We would also like to record our grateful appreciation to the League of Friends of the Atkinson Morley's Hospital who stimulated us to write this book, and who so generously restored the grave of Mr. Atkinson Morley in Highgate Cemetery to mark the one hundred and twenty fifth anniversary of his hospital's foundation in 1994. Finally, we would wish to thank Christine Saunders who helped us with the typing of the manuscript. We hope that this book will serve both as a reminder and as a partial repayment of the debt that St. George's Hospital in general and the neurosciences in particular owe to the generosity of Atkinson Morley.

1

The Early Years

In 1716 Henry Hoare, a merchant banker, William Wogan, a writer on religious subjects, Robert Witham, a brewer and Patrick Cockburn, a former curate met at St. Dunstan's Coffee House in Fleet Street and discussed the plight of the sick among the poor people of Westminster and decided to collect money, clothes, linen and food to help these unfortunates. Encouraged by the success of their efforts they were able, in short order, to establish the Westminster Public Infirmary in Petty France in 1720. The Infirmary which was supported entirely by voluntary contributions soon found itself in need of larger premises and these were opened in Chapel Street during 1724. By 1732 the Chapel Street establishment was found in turn to be inadequate for the growing needs of the charity, so its Vice-President, a Mr. Green, very generously offered two larger houses of his own for consideration which were situated in James Street and Castle Lane respectively. A majority of the governors favoured the house in Castle Lane, but a minority, which included most of the medical staff, preferred a third option namely that of Lanesborough House at Hyde Park Corner, which also happened to be available. The upshot being that whilst the majority agreed to take up Mr. Green's offer and adapt the Castle Lane premises, the obstinate minority decided that they would rather break away and open their own hospital at Hyde Park Corner. The arguments between the two groups grew in heat and acrimony, and ultimately entered the public domain. Several open letters were exchanged setting out the irreconcilable views of the protagonists. These were given a wide circulation and copies of them exist in the possession of the British Museum. Although the dispute was carried out with considerable bitterness and wide publicity which seemed to run directly counter to the philanthropic aims of the participants (a situation not entirely unknown to those familiar with charitable enterprises in our own times), the outcome, nevertheless, was enormously beneficial to the sick poor of London as it led to the establishment of two major voluntary hospitals: the Westminster, and St. George's.

Initially most of the surgeons and physicians who had favoured the move to Lanesborough House agreed to continue to serve the Westminster until it could appoint its own medical staff. Despite this additional heavy commitment the surgical and the medical staff attracted such large numbers of patients to the new hospital at Hyde Park Corner that in 1745 the original 30 beds had increased to over 250. (Imagine enterprise on this scale happening in the 'market culture' of the 1990s NHS!)

By the beginning of the nineteenth century the original building was no longer suitable for use as a hospital, in view of this a meeting of the Board of Governors in 1825 resolved that 'the accommodations of the present hospital are totally inadequate to the wants of the public'. Lewis Wyatt, the hospital architect was asked to draw up plans for a new 350 bedded hospital which he estimated would cost £50,000 to build. Alarmed at what was considered to be this huge expenditure, the Board decided to invite other architects to present designs, and, from these, the submission by William Wilkins who had designed both University College and the National Gallery was selected, which was costed at an estimated £40,000.

Building work began in 1827 and the new St. George's Hospital was completed in 1834 and only cost marginally more than Wilkins had originally estimated (cf. accuracy of late 20th century costings e.g. Charing Cross Hospital, British Library etc.), despite the fact that the builder was forced to charge an additional twelve hundred pounds when he found that part of the site had been previously excavated and filled with rubbish, which necessitated extra work in the shape of deeper foundations. This fine building continued in use as a hospital until 1980 when the present St. George's Hospital opened in Tooting. Within a period of less than thirty years from the opening of the Wilkins' designed building at Hyde Park Corner it was apparent that it could no longer cope with the rapid development of medical practice, or the needs of the patients for space and comfort. An attic floor designed by A. P. Mee was added between 1851 and 1859 to provide large cheerful rooms for the convalescent patients. But such were the insatiable demands for space by the medical staff that these rooms were in their turn very quickly used for other purposes: including an operating theatre, and additional wards for the acutely ill. The importance of convalescence despite being strongly advocated by leading writers in the *Medical Times and Gazette* was once again ignored. One of the staunchest supporters of the need for convalescence was one of the Governors of St. George's Hospital: Mr. Atkinson Morley. No first hand evidence has come to light to indicate why this new aspect of health care so appealed to him, but ever since he had been appointed a Governor in 1830 he had given, in addition to his annual subscription, a further £100 a year to the convalescent fund, and on his death he left a large legacy to St. George's Hospital so that it could go ahead and build its own independent convalescent hospital. Perhaps he was prompted by Charles Hawkins as one story would have it; in any event he could hardly fail to be moved by the noisesome squalor and ever present risk of disease which surrounded him: the cholera epidemic which broke out in 1848 claimed the lives of nearly 13,000 Londoners in the last three months of 1849; although pure speculation it is tempting to think that he may have been swayed by John Snow (of Broad Street pump fame) who was also a Governor of the hospital. The concept of a separate and dedicated hospital for the sole purpose of providing convalescent care was in those days unique. Thus it was that during the middle of the nineteenth century one of the most momentous and far-sighted developments in the history of St. George's Hospital occurred – the provision of a purpose built convalescent hospital. That it was developed in rural peace and seclusion at the edge of a beech wood, along a country lane on the outskirts of the village of Wimbledon is another story. It was not all plain sailing!

2

Atkinson Morley and his Will

The Atkinson Morley bequest to St. George's Hospital is recorded on the marble plaque which hangs in the Front Entrance of the Atkinson Morley's Hospital. It was sculpted in 1867 by John Gray Bedford at a cost of £62 and the discerning eye will notice that the sculptor made an error with the spelling of the word, 'calendar' at his first attempt. It reads :-

> Mr Atkinson Morley of Cork Street, Burlington Gardens, London, who died on the 14th July 1858 made certain bequests to his relatives and friends. Also, bequeathed the sum of five thousand pounds, to found in University College, London, the Atkinson Morley surgical scholarships, the interest on three thousand pounds to be annually divided among ten widows of tradesmen of St. James', Westminster, to be called the Atkinson Morley's Widows' Fund. To Queen Charlotte's Lying-in-Hospital, the Lock Hospital, St. Mary's Hospital, London, and the Royal Sea-Bathing Infirmary, Margate, one thousand pounds each, and 'directed that the residue of his property should accumulate for five years, and then be applied to the building and the endowing of a Hospital or a house of reception, with suitable gardens and grounds, for the purpose of receiving and maintaining, and generally assisting the convalescent poor patients from St. George's Hospital, until they shall be restored to strength and health, but that no such patient shall continue in such hospital for a period exceeding six calendar months; the property, and the exclusive control and management of the convalescent hospital, to be vested in the corporation of St. George's Hospital, to be called Atkinson Morley's Convalescent Hospital.

Who was this eponymous benefactor? And why did he leave his fortune to St. George's Hospital? According to Boase's *Modern English Biography* Atkinson Morley was born in 1781, but it is not recorded where this event took place. In Victorian times it was not unusual for mothers to register births in their home towns or villages. However, it is likely that Atkinson Morley was born in London as his father, David Morley, a coffeeman, had purchased the lease of the British Coffee House on the 1st July 1777. The British Coffee House had been founded in 1702 at an address which was described as 'opposite Suffolk Street' or 'over against the King's Mews in Charing Cross'. Coffee houses served many purposes, including those of a social club, an hotel, a place of business, a newsroom and often a library. It will be recalled that it was at St. Dunstan's Coffee House where the discussions were held which led eventually to the foundation of St. George's Hospital.

The British Coffee House along with Buttons, Slaughters, the St. James', the Bedford, Lloyds, Dick and Wills was a well known and popular meeting place for judges, architects, writers, actors and doctors. It was equally renowned for its hospitable welcome to socially disposed Scots who lived in or travelled to London, probably because it was invariably kept by a Scottish woman in its earlier days. Daniel Defoe was prompted to remark in 1720 that 'the Scots go generally to the British'. Indeed, one of its earliest visitors was James Erskine who became one of the Supreme Judges of Scotland (as Lord Grange) but resigned to become a member of parliament in order to oppose Walpole. His visits to London were enhanced by his love for the landlady of the British Coffee House – Fanny Lindsey – who had succeeded Mrs Anne Fenwick as the chatelaine of the establishment in 1728. This affair led to matrimonial disharmony, so he arranged for Lord Lovat to abduct Lady Grange in January 1732 and imprison her on St. Kilda's where she remained for seven years. She was still a prisoner at the time of her death in 1745 on the Isle of Skye. Grange had celebrated her 'funeral' in 1732 and years later married Fanny, his political career was effectively over when he violently opposed the abolition of the Witchcraft Acts in 1734; he died in obscurity and poverty in 1754. Lovat was an unmitigated scoundrel, who, although escaping punishment for this dreadful crime, was ultimately beheaded on Tower Hill in 1747 for bringing his Clan out in support of the

Jacobites two years earlier. There were many other colourful characters who frequented the British, and other young Scots included Tobias Smollett, a struggling surgeon who became a well known literary figure, Alexander Carlyle who became Minister of Inveresk and an important contributor to the political polemics of his time, John Blair, a future prebendary of Westminster, and Robert Smith who later was appointed as Master of Trinity College, Cambridge. By the middle of the eighteenth century, the British Coffee House was used by such notables as Robert Adam, the architect who designed the Adelphi and was responsible for the redesigned Drury Lane Theatre, David Garrick, the actor, Drs. Armstrong and Pitcairn from St. Bartholomew's Hospital and William Hunter, the famous anatomist and elder brother of John Hunter, the father of modern scientific surgery and St. George's most illustrious pupil and surgeon. The 'British' was also used for Masonic Lodge meetings at this time. In 1770 the British Coffee House was rebuilt by Robert Adam and its address was then given precisely as 27 Cockspur Street. Samuel Johnson, Oliver Goldsmith, James Boswell and John Wilkes all frequented the refurbished coffee house and continued to do so after it was purchased by David Morley. Under his direction the reputation of the British Coffee House grew steadily, and in 1803 it was described as 'remarkable for good breakfast and jellies'.

In the 1809–1811 directories, the House is listed as the British Coffee House and Wine Merchants and also as the British Hotel, now under the ownership of David and his wife. Under their joint proprietorship it is recorded in 1815 that the British Hotel was renowned for its fine wines.

As the prospect of consuming good breakfasts and fine wines in convivial company continued to attract the professional classes and the intelligentsia to its tables, so it seems safe to assume that, although details of Atkinson Morley's childhood remain obscure, he, his three brothers Samuel, David, John and his sister, Mary would have met a number of eminent doctors, writers, judges and actors who visited his father's coffee house. It is possible that such intimate encounters with the medical establishment stimulated the young Atkinson Morley's interest in medicine, or perhaps he was subjected to indirect parental influences, but in any event he seems to have embarked on a career in medicine.

At the time of his death in 1858, the *Medical Times and Gazette* stated that he was a medical student at St. George's Hospital in the early part of the century, but left medicine to become one of the most successful of London's hotel keepers. There is no record of Atkinson Morley ever having been a pupil of St. George's in the hospital's 'Pupil Registers', but he did bequeath some surgical instruments to his friend and an executor of his Will, William James Braine, an established surgeon. The question remains open as to how he came by these instruments. Did he purchase them in adult life as a result of his intense interest in matters medical, or did he acquire them to impress as an enthusiastic youngster when he set out on his career in medicine as, perhaps, a pupil at one of the independent anatomy schools such as Hunter's School of Anatomy in Great Windmill Street?

What sort of a world did Atkinson Morley inhabit? When he was born George III was on the throne, and in November of 1781 came unwelcome news to British shores. A major defeat for British troops had just occurred at the hands of the American colonists fighting for their freedom from the yoke of the British Parliament and its power to tax. This debacle at Yorktown marked the turning point in the British fortunes in the American War of Independence which ended in 1783 with the colonists seceding from the Crown. He went on to live under three other monarchs: George IV, William IV, and Victoria; and saw in his lifetime the demise of the *Ancien Regime* during the French revolution, the Napoleonic Wars, and the widening and deepening of the democratic institutions of British life.

There is no doubt that Atkinson Morley counted among his many friends several eminent medical men. William Joseph Goodwin, James William Braine and Samuel Armstrong Lane, all doctors, were named as executors of his Will, which was written on the 4th of July, 1856. All three had been pupils of St. George's Hospital and all had studied anatomy at Hunter's school so it is just possible that Atkinson Morley first made their acquaintance at Great Windmill Street, and, as a result, they all remained lifelong friends. Braine became Atkinson Morley's personal physician in later years. Samuel Armstrong Lane was closely associated with St. George's Hospital. He was born in 1802 and had enrolled as a pupil under Sir Everard Home in 1821 and became a perpetual pupil in 1822 in order to become a house surgeon in the fullness of time. He was taught anatomy at Great Windmill Street by James Wilson. After completing his studies in Edinburgh and Paris under Dupytrens and Magendie, Lane was elected a house surgeon at St. George's in 1827. His consuming ambition was to be elected to the honorary staff of the hospital, and, probably, in an attempt to ensure that he achieved his goal he opened his school of anatomy at 1 Grosvenor Place in 1830. Lane's school was known as 'The School of Anatomy and Medicine adjoining St. George's Hospital' and was a direct descendant of Hunter's school and probably the last of the private schools. The school received its students from St. George's, and quite naturally many of the lecturers were on the staff of the hospital, among them was Lane's friend and colleague, the son of his former anatomy teacher, James Arthur Wilson, commonly known as 'Maxilla' on account of his initials. This friendship was to prove disastrous for Lane's career ambitions. James Arthur Wilson, a physician at St. George's, and Benjamin Brodie disliked each other intensely. It was rumoured that their vitriolic hatred for each other had arisen from some pecuniary dispute between Brodie and Wilson's father. Whatever the cause of their disagreement, the mutual antipathy that festered between Brodie and Wilson ruined Lane's bid to become a surgeon at St. George's. When the vacancy for the post of a second Assistant Surgeon occurred in 1834 and Lane put his name forward with the support of Wilson, Brodie canvassed the Governors and the remainder of the medical staff to vote for Edward Cutler. Brodie's open support of Cutler, and his defamation of Lane for no apparent reason other than Lane's association with Wilson was the talk of medical circles in London and was even reported in the newspapers. Poor Lane was the victim of a campaign of systematic vilification, he was ostracised, and as a consequence Cutler was elected to the post by 178 votes to 99. Two years later Brodie purchased a house in Kinnerton Street so that the medical staff could open their own medical school. For the next twenty years the two schools, Lanes' and the one in Kinnerton Street coexisted, and although several attempts were made to amalgamate them, none succeeded because of the animosity between the two sides. In 1868 the Kinnerton Street School moved into a new building in Knightsbridge adjacent to the hospital and became known as the Medical School of St. George's Hospital. Soon after this occurred Lane was elected surgeon to St. Mary's Hospital and closed his school in Grosvenor Place. Atkinson Morley was a governor at St. George's throughout this period. It would be interesting to know which side he supported but one cannot help feeling that if William Goodwin was correct in a statement he made after Morley's death it seems clear that the latter would have supported Samuel Lane unreservedly, and been strongly opposed to Brodie's machinations. Atkinson Morley clearly had a great respect for Lane because he entrusted him to help with the execution of his will. There is no doubt that the legacy of £1,000 to St. Mary's Hospital was given solely on account of his friendship with Lane. Nevertheless, for reasons that are unclear to us, Atkinson Morley continued his support for St. George's Hospital until in due course it acquired the major part of his estate.

Another medical friend of Atkinson Morley was Robert Liston, the University College Hospital surgeon who achieved fame on 21 December 1846 when he amputated the leg of Frederick Churchill, a 36 year old builder under an ether anaesthetic which was given by a 21 year old medical student, William Squire, whose uncle Peter, the Queen's chemist and druggist, had designed the inhaler used. After the leg had been painlessly removed Liston turned to the observers and remarked, 'This Yankee dodge, gentlemen, beats mesmerism hollow'. Liston died of a ruptured aortic aneurysm one year later. Morley described Liston in his Will as his friend and companion.

The evidence for these cordial relations rests in the fact that Morley had received a silver snuff box as a gift from Liston at some point, which later he bequeathed to Robert Gadsden. Liston also lent Morley a valuable oil painting which was hung in the lounge of Morley's Hotel. On his death, Morley set up trust funds for both Liston's widow, Christine and her youngest daughter, Marian. The University College Hospital scholarships almost certainly came about because of the close friendship between Liston and Morley.

Morley might well have made such friends as a medical student, or equally their friendships may have developed after he had entered and promoted the family business. In 1822, when Atkinson Morley was forty one years of age, he is listed as the owner of the British Hotel at 25

Cockspur Street; so now he was in charge of the family's hotel business, which had earlier sold the British Coffee House at 27 Cockspur Street to a John Clements. Atkinson Morley, soon disposed of the British Hotel and purchased in its place the Burlington Hotel at 19-20 Cork Street. In 1831 he must have felt sufficiently secure financially to build the Morley's Hotel at 1-3 Trafalgar Square. With its one hundred rooms this elegant early nineteenth century building became one of London's most prestigious hotels and prospered until 1921 when it was demolished to make way for the present South Africa House.

It was from these business enterprises that Atkinson Morley amassed the fortune he used to such generous effect in his support of charitable work. Atkinson Morley became a governor of St. George's Hospital in 1830 and, in addition to his annual subscription of over ten guineas, he contributed £100 a year to the convalescent fund, which he continued to do for the remainder of his life. We do not know the reason for Atkinson Morley's special interest in convalescence. It is most unlikely that he was ever treated personally in St. George's which has been given as a reason for his concern by some writers, because as a man of considerable substance he would not have chosen to be treated in a voluntary hospital. The most likely scenario is that he was persuaded of the beneficial powers of convalescence by his first hand knowledge of the hospital and its patients, possibly his solicitude was aroused by the problems suffered by one of his own servants, who would have been entitled to treatment at the hospital by virtue of Morley's governship. He may have recounted to Morley how disagreeable the noise and the smoke at Hyde Park Corner were, making it virtually impossible to rest and recover in these circumstances. It would not take Morley long to work out the potential benefits to members of his staff of a stay in the country to recuperate after an operation or illness.

Morley never married and died on the 14th July 1858 at the age of 77 years, according to his death certificate, from 'paralysis and exhaustion of old age'. According to his wishes he was buried in Highgate Cemetery on the 20th July 1858. St. George's was notified of the contents of Atkinson Morley's '13-Page Will' within a few weeks of his death, but as it was to be five years before the Hospital would derive the full benefit of the accumulated funds, planning for the new hospital proceeded slowly and with exemplary caution as there was a clause in Atkinson Morley's will which forbade St. George's from interfering in any way with the execution of his last wishes.

Although details of the development crept along at snail's pace, the five years period was not uneventful in human terms, and within a very short time there were angry differences, both private and public, between the executors and St. George's Hospital; and then later the executors quarrelled amongst themselves. All three executors were left £500 each for their pains under the terms of the Will, but soon after its publication Braine claimed that he had paid 3,501 professional visits to Atkinson Morley over a ten years period and according to him 'most of these involved necessary surgical operations carried out at both day and night'. This works out at the astonishing figure of almost a visit a day, and if each attendance involved some sort of surgical service it is scarcely surprising that convalescence would be uppermost in Morley's mind, as he must surely have been in desperate need for some himself! Braine also claimed to have arranged twelve consultations with other physicians and surgeons – a paltry number bearing in mind the duration of symptoms and his own obsequious attentions. For all this professional service he claimed he was owed £4,464-12s.

Mr. Roger Gadsden, Morley's solicitor, who was named as trustee for the affairs of the Hotel in the Will, claimed that he was still owed £1,477-11s for professional services he had rendered to Morley. In addition, Charles Foster, the head waiter of Morley's Hotel petitioned for the payment of £475, a sum which he said Morley had promised him but which had never been forthcoming.

Dilatoriness in the presentation of accounts is not unknown in professional circles, but, not unreasonably, both Lane and Goodwin felt that these delays were excessive, and that the bills should have been settled during Morley's lifetime so they appealed to the governors of St. George's for guidance. The hospital refused to interfere for fear that any intervention on its part would nullify the terms of the will, and thereby forfeit the legacy. Lane and Goodwin applied to the Court of Chancery to administer the estate. Sir John Stuart, the Vice-Chancellor, decided that all of these claims should be paid in full. This judgement riled Goodwin and Lane who both felt that the hospital should have joined with them in opposing payment. Goodwin, also a governor of St. George's, wrote to the Hospital and to the Daily Telegraph. Goodwin reminded the governors of St. George's Hospital that in 1849 when they were asked to pay the £275 a year to Sir Benjamin Brodie for the use of his house in Kinnerton Street as a medical school Atkinson Morley had been very much opposed to the use of the charity's moneys for the purpose of professional education, but being too ill to state his case in person he had sent Goodwin along to the Board meeting in his place, where the latter expressed Morley's opposition to the Board, but his comments were ignored, and they agreed to go ahead and pay the rent. Goodwin claimed that Atkinson Morley was so incensed by this slight that he immediately changed his Will excluding St. George's Hospital as a beneficiary, which left him very much surprised when the will was read to find that Morley had altered it yet again and reinstated the hospital as the major benefactor. Goodwin also said 'it is well known that he (Morley) was always complaining of the influence of the medical officers being prejudicial to the hospital's welfare and he often adverted to the anomaly of their being virtually their own masters when voting upon all questions concerning their own interests'. This barbed remark was undoubtedly aimed at Brodie, certainly over the Kinnerton Street rent, but it could have alluded equally well to Brodie's spoiling tactics at the time of the election for the assistant surgeon.

In the next escalation of the dispute Goodwin publicly accused the hospital of sharp practice by advertising regularly for donations to the detriment of other hospitals when recently it had been endowed by Sir Thomas Apreece's generous legacy of £91,000, and would also stand to gain considerably from the Morley legacy.

Turning then to the testament itself Goodwin argued that under the terms of Morley's Will only £50,000 of the legacy was to be spent on the building of a convalescent hospital, with the remainder to be made available for the general purposes of St. George's Hospital, and he accused St. George's Hospital of deliberately attempting to misconstrue those terms so that it could appropriate the whole of the £150,000 for the provision of a convalescent hospital.

Thomas Nettleship, the hospital solicitor, was anxious to respond, but first took counsel's advice and was told by his barrister, Mr. Swainton

QC, not to respond to Goodwin's accusations. Nettleship, however, was sufficiently provoked to reply to an anonymously written paragraph in *Bells Life* that included part of Goodwin's letter which centred mainly around a Mr. Bank who had persuaded the Jockey Club to donate ten percent of the takings from the Oaks and the Derby to half a dozen charities, of which St. George's Hospital was one. Nettleship replied that the paper had been misled by Goodwin, that Morley's intentions were absolutely clear in stating that his legacy should be used solely for the establishment and maintenance of a convalescent institution, and that it could not be used for the general purposes of St. George's Hospital. He went on 'your strictures are unfounded and calculated to injure St. George's Hospital'. The Editor added 'we recollect Mr. Goodwin telling us that £50,000 as a competent part thereof was to be expended on the convalescent hospital and that the rest would go into the general fund of St. George's Hospital. We have no doubt, however, that Mr. G. will set us and the public right in the matter and our readers will then be able to judge whether our strictures are unfounded'.

Samuel Lane, who had every reason to bear a grudge against St. George's but never openly showed it, added a small protest by way of claiming damages for the down draught it had created on his property in Tattersall's Yard, now Grosvenor Mews, by the recent addition of an attic floor designed by A.P. Mee.

Nevertheless, in spite of the divisive efforts of the contestors, there was nothing they could do to prevent compliance with Atkinson Morley's last wishes.

The five years wait for capital appreciation was a difficult and frustrating period, but during it St. George's saw its promised legacy eventually becoming a reality, and planning for the convalescent hospital was able to go ahead. Possible sites on which to build the convalescent hospital were sought by Charles Hawkins, the Treasurer of St. George's Hospital. As a matter of interest Charles Hawkins, who was a superb surgeon and an assistant as well as a friend of Brodie, was widely tipped to become the successor to Thomas Tatum as assistant surgeon to St. George's in 1843, but lost the election to a less well-qualified candidate, Henry Charles Johnson, probably because the governors wished to assert their independence of medical opinion, and were fearful lest they might be accused again of being under Brodie's thumb, as they had been in the case of Cutler nearly ten years previously. This short sighted approach to appointments did nothing to enhance the reputation of the hospital, and dealt a savage blow to the ambitions of a uniquely gifted surgeon. It speaks volumes for Hawkins' character that he was able to overcome this disappointment, and go on to fulfil himself as one of the greatest servants of St. George's Hospital, whose destiny it was to be largely responsible for the establishment of Atkinson Morley's Hospital. Hawkins drew up a list of twenty four possible sites for the convalescent hospital, and out of these four were short listed, after being identified as potentially the most suitable. According to Atkinson Morley's wishes the hospital had to be within seven miles of Hyde Park Corner, but the Governors of St. George's would have preferred a ten to twelve miles radius to ensure a complete change of air.

The four sites selected for consideration were:

1. 40 acres at Caterham at a cost of £4,200.
2. 37 acres in Nightingale Lane, Clapham Common priced at £3,500.
3. 28 acres on Mr. Bates' estate at Sheen, for which he wanted £2,500.
4. 40 acres on Lord Cottenham's Estate in Wimbledon at a cost of £3,500.

A surveyor was instructed to recommend the most suitable site and after careful examination he concluded that Wimbledon was the best option. The medical officers of St. George's Hospital, Messrs. Page, Pitman, Fuller, Pollock, Holmes and Ogle, were invited to give their views which resulted in the rather pompous statement that 'Wimbledon would be unsuitable if the soil is not fully and completely drained. Also, the proximity of the site to London rendered the locality liable during the prevalence of the east wind to have the air tainted with the smoke of the metropolis and possible with a south or west wind the damp rising from the valley would be objectionable'.

Fortunately, the Board, although noting these comments, instructed the solicitors to take the necessary steps to secure the land and a portion of the Cottenham Estate was purchased. What was this estate and how did it come to be on the market? In fact progressive development of the land had taken place over the previous hundred years, and it was only towards the end of this period that it became known as the Cottenham Estate. Originally Peter Taylor, a goldsmith had built 'Prospect Place', a large mansion, on a six acre plot in 1757 and this was situated just to the east of where the present Hospital now sits. It gained its name 'Prospect Place' from its extensive panoramic views to the south. Moses Isaac Levy purchased the estate in 1767 and laid out the gardens. James Meyrick, a parliamentary agent took possession of the house and grounds around 1792 and purchased an additional 250 acres of surrounding land which he had partly landscaped at great expense by Humphrey Repton and the remainder he used for agricultural purposes. When Meyrick died the estate was purchased at auction in 1825 by John Lambton who after serving in the Dragoons had been returned as a Whig M.P. for Durham in 1813 and proved to be one of the leading reformers of his day. He was created Baron Durham in 1828, and, in the administration of his father-in-law Lord Grey, he was made Lord Privy Seal. Lambton sold 'Prospect Place' in 1831 and shortly after in 1833 he resigned from office, when he was made an Earl. Although his active political career was over he continued to serve his country; firstly, as ambassador-extraordinary to St. Petersburg, after which he became Governor-General of Canada. The new owner of the Wimbledon estate was a leading barrister named Charles Pepys, who was a direct descendant of the famous diarist Samuel Pepys. Charles Pepys, another Whig, entered parliament and in turn became Solicitor-General, Master of the Rolls, and finally Lord Chancellor, taking the title of Lord Cottenham in doing so. He was said to be an intensely shy person, who claimed that, on arrival home after a day's work, nothing gave him greater delight than to rush up to the nursery and sing to his children, this would give enormous scope to his vocal repertoire as he had no less than 15 children. After losing office for a time, he was restored to his previous position in 1846, but he proved to be much less successful than he had been during his original period of tenure; the reason for this lay in the fact that he had become virtually unintelligible due to the loss of all his teeth, not a suitable qualification for the head of the country's legal system. Despite this it was clear that he had forfeited none of his personal popularity because his colleagues were anxious to club together to purchase a pair of false teeth for him, but he declined their kind offer and struggled on for a little longer before relinquishing his high office. On the domestic front he made a number of improvements to the estate which included making new entrances and drives as well as introducing an experimental farm. On Cottenham's death in 1851 the estate was divided up with most of the land being sold to developers, but 'Prospect Place' including 40 acres of land was acquired by the second Duke of Wellington who unfortunately lacked the same keen interest in the property as its previous owners, and he lived in the house for only a few years before he left it vacant. In 1863 the now dilapidated 'Prospect Place' and attached land was purchased by a Mr. Sims who demolished the house before selling off 28 acres of the land to St. George's Hospital.

St. George's enlisted Messrs. Kelly and Crawley of Thavies Inn as architects and together they drew up plans for the Atkinson Morley's Hospital. Messrs. Simpsons, the builders of Baker Street were asked to complete the building and the foundation stone of the Atkinson Morley's Convalescent Hospital was laid on Friday 19th July 1867 by Earl Cadogan. Messrs. Easton and Amos undertook all the engineering work, and a Mr. Potter of South Molton Street installed 'the apparatus of warming'. The completed building costing less than £24,000 was described in *The Lancet* of July 17th. 1869 as a 'handsome brick building' was formally opened on the 14th July 1869 exactly eleven years after the death of Atkinson Morley. The same edition of *The Lancet* congratulated the Governors of St. George's Hospital 'in having thus carried out the wishes of the benevolent founder of the Atkinson Morley Convalescent Hospital; and we feel sure that both they and the poor who will enjoy the benefits of the institution will appreciate the energy and skill with which the treasurer, Mr. Charles Hawkins, has brought the entire business to a successful issue'. The remainder of the Morley legacy was kept separately as the Atkinson Morley's Fund, to be used for the upkeep of the Hospital.

There were no fanfares or festivities at the official opening of the Hospital which was a very modest affair and consisted of a short religious service in the chapel. Refreshments were not provided in an attempt to save money. This muted approach to matters appeared justified because soon after the formal opening several ceilings in the wards and chapel area collapsed due to poor plaster work, thus the opening of the Hospital for admissions was delayed for several months. It was later discovered that several aspects of the building were defective, but this was not the fault of the builders: it was the Board of Governors who, while conscious of their collective public responsibilities, had been parsimonious to a marked degree, and were thus to blame by keeping the building costs pared to the bone.

A couple of years after the hospital opened it was realised by the Board of Governors that they did not possess the building plans. Mr Kelly had by now retired, and for reasons which are not clear Mr Crawley was loathe to hand over a set of the drawings. Eventually, and only after a good deal of persuasion, was Mr Crawley induced to hand over to the Governors a set which he claimed had to be redrawn, as the actual construction of the hospital differed greatly from the original design. It is odd that the Governors never questioned Mr Crawley as to the extent or the detail of these putative alterations!

3

The Atkinson Morley's Convalescent Hospital

The new Convalescent Hospital – Atkinson Morley's was built standing back from a narrow leafy lane, the western extension of an ancient trackway and drove road known as the Ridgeway connecting the village of Wimbledon with Kingston, which eventually became known as Copse Hill. The Wimbledon of those days was a vastly different place to the one we know now. By the middle of the nineteenth century Wimbledon was beginning to lose much of its rural seclusion. The advent of the railway in 1838 had brought it within daily commuting distance of the metropolis, but for a time little changed. The Ridgeway had seen a series of large villas spring up on either side of it. These were labour intensive habitations for members of the minor aristocracy, wealthy merchant princelings or senior members of the professional middle class, who lived leisured, pampered lives, serviced by a horde of other workers. These members of the lower orders had their own hierarchy of employment which covered indoor domestic duties, the gardens, and the horses which were still very much central to the heart of the transport system; and from these major branches sprang a host of subsidiary ones. Large numbers of workers were required to live locally to make sure that all these undertakings were managed smoothly and efficiently. Where better for them to live than at the bottom of the escarpment, south of the railway? This area saw rapid growth in the middle years of the century, and their numbers were augmented by railway workers and employees in other industries. Speculators were also busy on the north side of the railway on the slope of the hill, where land used for agricultural and horticultural purposes was divided up into building plots for increasing numbers of middle class dwellings; and gradually this process extended towards Copse Hill; though at the time of the hospital went up only the three mansions to the east of it existed, and they had been completed as recently as the 1850's.

As if to emphasise its lonely setting the hospital sheltered behind imposing wrought iron gates which guarded its entrance. These gates were normally kept closed and only opened on important occasions such as when consultants or governors arrived by hansom cab from Wimbledon Station to make their visits. Through the gates to the right was the small brick built lodge house on one wall of which was placed a disproportionately large clock. The first occupants of the lodge house were a Mr. and Mrs. Harding. Mr. Harding acted as the general factotum to the Hospital, and his wife performed general duties in the hospital but at times she deputised for the cook. At yearly intervals the hospital closed for one month for cleaning and re-decoration and the Hardings were responsible for this maintenance work. The remainder of the staff took their annual holiday during this period.

Entrance to the hospital was gained through a very fine portico which was sadly removed in the 1950's and replaced by an ugly canopy which affords some protection from the elements to those patients arriving or leaving by ambulance. Beyond the doors into the hospital was the entrance hall. To the left was the superintendent's dining room where the new small chapel is now situated and to the right was the boardroom. Behind the entrance hall was a very imposing large galleried chapel which in 1993 was converted into a lecture theatre. Rooms to the left and right of the corridors which flanked the chapel served as the vestry and dispensary. The floors of the passages and corridors were tiled and the walls were of stone. All the floors in the patient areas were kept on the same level – an unusually thoughtful provision for those days. The general plan of the hospital was in the shape of a flattened T and the area of the hospital described above formed the upright of the T. The elongated cross bar of the T on the south side of the hospital served as the ward or dormitory, day and delivery room areas for patients, all apart from the central part of the ground floor opposite to the chapel which served as the living quarters for the superintendent. To the right of the superintendent's accommodation were the male, large 20-bedded and the small 5-bedded wards, and to the left the same lay-out of accommodation for female patients.

On the floor above, which now houses the psychiatric wards, were two large 20-bedded wards and 10 small single bedded rooms, five male and five female. The area above the Superintendent's accommodation was used as the linen room and the rooms above that were used as bedrooms for the head nurse, assistant nurses and the servants. The head nurse was given her own bedroom, but the other 12 staff were forced to share the remaining three rooms.

Each of the large wards contained a double open fireplace with very ornamental flues and these were used to heat the water both for domestic purposes and to run the rudimentary central heating system. The walls were tiled up to six feet above the floor, and the windows extended from three feet above the floor to within one foot of the ceiling. Dirty linen and refuse was removed from the ward by 'chutes' directed into the basement, and a room was set aside for fumigating the bed linen. The basement floor contained separate dining rooms for the men and women, and day rooms which led into an outside open corridor where the patients could exercise. Also in the basement were the pantry, larder, scullery, porters' and servants' rooms, as well as the cellar, coal stores and the kitchen which was equipped with one of the Warren patent stoves 'similar to those used in the army by which food for the inmates will be cooked'. By then obsolete the coal stores were used during the 1950's – 70's as the doctors' dining room. Coal was poured through the 'chute entrances', which can still be seen on each side of the main entrance, into the store, from where it was transported to the wards for burning in the fireplaces.

The tower housed the large water tank. Access to the top of the tower was gained as it is today by a steep wooden staircase. The top of the tower remains a superb vantage point commanding magnificent views to the south. The tower and the southern aspect of the hospital stands out as a landmark and can be seen from many miles away. The northern aspect of the hospital remains less imposing as a large part of it is concealed behind the large earth bank which was formed when the site was levelled for building to commence in 1867.

At that time the area around the hospital was much more heavily wooded, indeed opposite the gates there was a beech wood, and the hospital grounds themselves contained more trees than is the case today (some fine specimens were lost in the hurricane of 1987), so the governors of the day erected a number of seats in the grounds on which the convalescent patients could sit and rest after their walks to enjoy watching the birds and other wildlife.

At the time of the hospital's construction the opportunity was taken to build a large laundry in its grounds. It was intended that this laundry would not only be capable of washing the dirty linen of the convalescent wards, but also that from the main hospital at Hyde Park Corner. In time it was realised that it could not cope with the demands of an expanding workload, but the laundry building survives to this day and can be seen to the east of the hospital where it is now used as a storeroom. Close to the laundry, but further east again, stood the old coach house and stables which was built to stable the horses and house the carriage which conveyed both patients and laundry to and from Hyde Park Corner.

The water supply to the hospital was provided initially by the Water Company but an artesian well was sunk close to the laundry which could furnish the combined needs of the hospital and the laundry quite comfortably, thus enabling the supply from the Utility to be discontinued with financial savings to the hospital. The sewage from the hospital was drained into a large reservoir which was placed in the large garden in the lower part of the grounds which was let to a market gardener who then used it as a fertiliser. The rain water was not allowed to mix with the sewage and was drained into a separate pond in another part of the grounds which was left as meadowland and eventually let as grazing to a Mr. Baring.

When finally completed Atkinson Morley's Convalescent Hospital was equipped with first class facilities with which to provide the highest standards of care for those inner city patients needing convalescence after inpatient medical or surgical treatment for serious illness at St. George's Hospital, and it was the envy of the other voluntary hospitals in London.

As soon as the faulty plasterwork was repaired the hospital opened its doors to receive patients in the autumn of 1869. Patients and laundry were transported from Hyde Park Corner to the Atkinson Morley's Hospital in two horse drawn black closed carriages on Wednesday afternoons.

Patrick Fawcett recalls in his *Memories of a Wimbledon childhood 1906-1918*, '. . . these buses were eventually motorised but up to at least 1915 they were each drawn by two horses and if we were indoors it was the clatter of their hooves approaching that would make us rush to the windows to be the first to see them pass'. The coachman wore a dark blue frock coat with a red collar and St. George's brass buttons made by Simpsons who made similar uniforms for the porters at Hyde Park Corner. As the coachman was exposed to the elements in winter he was provided with a 'box cloth' blue overcoat again with the distinctive red collar and brass buttons. Recognising that the coat received heavy wear the Governors agreed that the coachman should have a new one each year. However, the coachman did not have things all his own way, because very soon he was given a 'Time Book' in which he had to record his departure and arrival times. Also he was disciplined when he cut the corner on entering the grounds of Atkinson Morley's and damaged the gates!

The journey between the two hospitals would have taken quite a while and one can imagine the gamut of emotions that ran unbidden through the patients' minds as they left their familiar territory of Central London and travelled out into the countryside of Wimbledon. The most common would be: relief at having made a satisfactory recovery (so far); apprehension concerning the future; domestic anxieties; and how much they would miss their relatives until the coach made its return journey.

When they arrived at the Atkinson Morley's Convalescent Hospital they were greeted by Mr. John Gregory Smith, Fellow of the Royal College of Surgeons and Member of the Society of Apothecaries – the first Medical Superintendent, or 'Master' as he was commonly known. Gregory Smith who had qualified at St. George's in 1829 had lectured on surgery and anatomy with Prescott Hewett at the Great Windmill Street School for ten years before practising as a surgeon at the Marylebone General Dispensary. In 1844 he was elected a Fellow of the Royal College of Surgeons and he then moved to Harewood near Leeds where he practised until he was appointed to the Atkinson Morley's Convalescent Hospital. Gregory Smith's wife acted as matron and escorted the patients to their beds. The Gregory Smiths were jointly paid a salary of £250 per year but they were provided with free board and lodging. John Gregory Smith who was appointed for five years, was solely responsible for the medical care of the patients and the general running upkeep of the hospital, which included such tasks as purchasing a horse for £35, and selling a pig for £4. Gregory Smith was accountable to the Board of Governors of St. George's Hospital through the Atkinson Morley's Management Committee which was at first chaired by Charles Hawkins. The remainder of the committee was constituted of the treasurers, two members of the Medical Committee who were nominated annually, and twelve Governors who were elected by ballot. Although this Management Committee appointed a Chaplain, it was the matron who was usually acknowledged to be in charge of the spiritual as well as the physical well-being of both the patients and nurses, and attendance at chapel services was obligatory for all. Despite these apparently Draconian powers the matron was granted precious little freedom in the employment of staff, their leave, and what would now be called their conditions of service.

Besides the Gregory Smiths and the Hardings, other, additional, staff were employed: a Head Nurse, three Assistant Nurses, one undertaking night duties, a cook, a kitchen maid and the Engineman. Terms of employment were determined by the Management Committee. Such strict and rigorous management meant that costs were kept to a minimum, and in 1881 the wages for the whole nursing staff for the year came to slightly over £100. Their new uniforms, which had just been introduced at that time, cost just under ten pounds in total.

The Atkinson Morley's Convalescent Hospital quickly established itself, and very soon patients began to appreciate the advantages of not being discharged directly back into the slums from St. George's Hospital until they were fully restored to good health by being given the opportunity to recover in airy, clean, grand, and spacious surroundings before returning to the dismal squalor of their normal lives.

They were well fed and received good care. The Management Committee agreed the daily menu for the patients, and a breakfast of home-baked bread and butter with tea was served at 8 a.m. Dinner was served at 1 p.m.: mutton, either roast, boiled or hashed was served on four days in he week, and beef either roast or hashed was served on the remaining three days. Each was served with locally grown vegetables, and was followed by either suet or rice pudding. For those unfortunates who could not eat meat, soup and pudding was made available. Male patients were served with a pint of beer, females: a half, and children: a quarter. Bread and butter with tea was served at 5 p.m., and at 8 p.m. they were given a light supper of bread and cheese washed down with half a pint of beer, the children had to make do with bread and milk. The first patient was admitted on 13th October 1869 and it soon it worked out that one in every six patients treated at St. George's Hospital was sent to Wimbledon for convalescence. By the end of 1869, 95 patients had been admitted to the Atkinson Morley's Convalescent Hospital, each having stayed for an average of about three weeks. 670 patients were admitted during 1870 so at the end of the year an assessment of the benefits of the Hospital could be made. Results show that :-

    407 retired quite well
    179 nearly so, much improved
     61 improved
      4 not improved
      8 left at their own desire
      6 dismissed for irregularity
      5 died

The weekly Board of St. George's Hospital congratulated itself by noting that 'it cannot but consider that the above is a very satisfactory proof of the beneficial working of the convalescent hospital'. Furthermore, the cost only amounted to £4,400 against an income of £5,250, a situation which even the most miserly Governor would applaud. An excellent beginning! Sadly the financial state of the hospital would not always remain so healthy, but it was abundantly clear that Atkinson Morley's munificence was at last beginning to benefit increasing numbers of the sick poor.

4

A Period of Consolidation: 1870–1900

When the hospital first opened there was a honeymoon period during which both John Gregory Smith and his wife worked enthusiastically to help the hospital fulfil the hopes invested in it, and the expectations it aroused. Their commitment was recognised, and they were thanked in lavish terms by the Board of Governors for their 'unwavering kindness to patients'. However fairly soon it became clear that the Gregory Smiths were running the hospital in their own authoritarian way: making decisions and taking responsibility beyond their remit. Even in their inaugural year Gregory Smith had been rebuked for keeping patients in too long, later the Medical School Committee urged that he should not deviate from the treatment prescribed by the referring doctors, and that he should continue to keep up the notes (a recurring problem!). Timothy Holmes, the surgeon who was a medical member of the management committee wrote a long report and concluded that he was 'interested in improving standards and seeing that rules were obeyed'. As a result the committee proposed a new management structure which would considerably reduce the good doctor's power and influence. By this time Gregory Smith was up in arms having taken serious offence at these proposals. He refused to have his wings clipped with the inevitable upshot being that the honeymoon was suddenly over. To his dismay he found that he had overplayed his hand disastrously, and in 1874 he and his wife were effectively dismissed, but in a last desperate attempt to salvage something from the deteriorating situation he tried to extract £50 in compensation for the use of his own utensils which he claimed was necessary whilst he was in post because the Governors had failed to adequately equip his accommodation. He was probably correct in his claim, the niggardliness of the Governors has been noted earlier, but by now he was not arguing from a position of strength. The compensation was refused, and on this rather absurd off-key note they left.

After the unlamented departure of the Gregory Smiths, Miss Kyle who had been the matron at Hyde Park Corner was appointed acting matron (surely something of a come down for her!), and Dr. R.T. Poole Collyns was appointed resident medical officer. In order to avoid a repetition of the Gregory Smith debacle the Governors decided to appoint a visiting surgeon and physician to advise the medical officer on the care of the patients. It is not a matter of great surprise to find that very soon it had became the custom for the most junior assistant physician and surgeon at St. George's to be appointed, at a salary of £100 a year, but as they gained seniority they would (unselfishly) relinquish the post in favour of the most recently appointed of their colleagues, who would don their vacated mantle, but count the days until they too would be able to lay down this rural burden – and spend a more profitable half-day in London. Some things never change!.

In 1874 the first visiting physician was appointed, Thomas Tillyer Whipham (1843-1917), who was born in London and educated at Rugby and Oriel College, Oxford, before entering St. George's Hospital as a student in 1864. After qualification he proceeded to his MD and was elected FRCP before being appointed as Assistant Physician in 1872 and then Physician four years later. Whipham, with his bushy grey beard and mutton chop whiskers, was very popular and was said to have been highly regarded by the nurses. Although thought by many to be 'deficient in the art of self assertion', he became Dean of the Medical School and Censor of the Royal College of Physicians (no mean feat for one so lacking in personal magnetism). It is said that he once advised his successor as curator of the museum 'don't despise your lunch – you will not care for it at first working in the museum, and will be inclined to give it away to someone, but you will be the better for it and will soon feel you want it'.

On his retirement in 1886 he moved to Hatherleigh in Devon where he was able to pursue his love for country life and angling.

Whipham's surgical counterpart was James Rouse (1830-1896), who was born in Fulham and entered St. George's Hospital as a student in 1845 under Caesar Hawkins. He became a member of the College of Surgeons in 1851 and because of his helpfulness to pupils when he was a house surgeon he was known ever after as 'The Old'un'. Rouse was appointed Associate Surgeon in 1867 and Surgeon in 1875. He had a major interest in ophthalmic surgery. With his black hair and large frame he had the appearance of a successful surgeon, but he was once described as a 'fat cheery man who did not penetrate the abdomen gladly'. A colleague Dr. Dickinson said of Rouse 'that I have never known him perform an unnecessary operation' but behind his back the reason for this became apparent as Dickinson described him as 'a surgeon we can control'.

In 1876 the Governors, who could be forgiven a brief respite on their laurels having satisfied themselves that they had sorted out the problems at Atkinson Morley's Hospital, were suddenly inundated by a new disaster, this time at Hyde Park Corner. Inundation is the *mot juste* in this case as the water tank on the roof burst and five thousand gallons of water cascaded down through the wards bearing four patients in their beds on a torrent of water into the Medical Students' sitting room on the ground floor. Normally one of the most densely populated areas in the hospital it was fortunate that only seven students were in the room when the accident happened. Dame Fortune continued to smile for only one was injured and this occurred when the young man jumped out of the window and sprained his ankle trying to avoid the flood – one would have thought he would have had the wit to go up rather than down to escape!. The patients fared less well, for not only had they been caught up in a harrowing calamity, but two of those injured in this episode subsequently died.

It was not long, however, before the Wimbledon hospital was back in the spotlight. The Atkinson Morley patients began to feel the effects of a cost cutting exercise, the very first of countless subsequent ones, which was introduced in order to reduce expenditure which was already exceeding income (where has this been heard before?). The mounting

29

costs had resulted from a considerable increase in the yearly admissions, the average for which was now running at about 800 per year. Amongst the belt-tightening measures introduced was a drastic reduction in the outlay on brandy from £51 to £7-14s a year. Savings were also made in cooking, fuel, furniture and bedding.

A small shift towards a more active clinical stance was now taking place at Wimbledon. Timothy Holmes, a St. George's surgeon was called in to undertake two amputations, but unfortunately both patients died, so it was considered inadvisable to undertake further surgery at the Atkinson Morley's Hospital. For the first time, boys under the age of 14 and girls under the age of 7 were admitted for convalescence. Also, at this time, one of the patients gave birth and this prompted the governors to ask Robert Barnes, the obstetrician as to how a pregnant lady came to be sent for convalescence. Barnes answered that he was uncertain whether the woman suffered from a tumour or was in fact pregnant, so he felt two to three weeks convalescence would help decide the matter one way or the other. With the arrival of the baby matters were very much decided and Barnes was consequently rebuked.

In 1874 James Rouse retired as visiting surgeon and was replaced by Mr. Thomas Pickering Pick (1841-1918). Pick, the son of a Liverpool merchant entered St. George's as a pupil in 1857, qualified MRCS and LSA in 1862 and obtained his FRCS in 1866. After qualification he undertook a number of appointments at St. George's Hospital in anatomy and surgery before being appointed Assistant Surgeon in 1869, Surgeon in 1878, and Consulting Surgeon in 1898 on his retirement. Pick edited Gray's *Anatomy* and Holmes' *Principles and Practice of Surgery*. He was well respected and recognised as a good teacher. Pick was described as 'a good looking man with wonderful early greying hair and a crisp and kindly manner'.

Pickering Pick became a member of the Council of the Royal College of Surgeons, going on to become Vice-President of the College and Emeritus Professor in 1894. His other appointments included surgeon to the Victoria Hospital for Children, Chelsea, and HM Inspector of Anatomy for England and Wales. Pick often illustrated his lectures with verses which he recited in his Liverpudlian accent. His lecture on amyloid disease always began with 'Mornin' Flushin', Evenin' Sweatin', Patient daily weaker gettin''. On retirement in 1898 he lived in Bookham, Surrey until his death in 1918. The photograph of Pickering Pick which is reproduced in this book was taken by Clinton Dent, later to become another visiting surgeon to the Atkinson Morley's.

A year after Pickering Pick was appointed Visiting Surgeon, John Cavafy took over as Visiting Physician from Thomas Whipham. John Cavafy (1837-1901) was the son of a Greek merchant and he worked for four years in his father's office before entering St. George's as a pupil in 1861. Cavafy obtained his Doctorate of Medicine in 1865 and became a Member of the Royal College of Physicians in 1868., From then on his promotion was rapid, he was elected Assistant Physician to St. George's Hospital in 1874 and advanced to full physician status in 1876. John Cavafy, bespectacled and bearded, favouring a black jacket and pin-striped trousers was of a severe mien but he had 'a claim of manner which endeared him to seniors and juniors alike'. Although a general physician he had a keen interest in diseases of the skin and took over the Department of Dermatology from Thomas Whipham in 1882. It was said that he was 'always clear, always emphatic, very rarely dogmatic, he had few equals as a teacher of medicine'. Underneath his austere, learned appearance John Cavafy, in his spare time a talented artist and musician, possessed a keen sense of humour and a ready wit. On one occasion as Mr. Rouse entered the front hall of the hospital carrying, as usual, his little black bag, the contents of which had always been a mystery to his colleagues, he bumped into Dr. Cavafy and said 'Now Dr. Cavafy, I shouldn't mind making you a small bet that you don't tell me what I've got in this bag'. 'I shouldn't wonder if there was a stethoscope', was the instant, ready, and correct reply. John Cavafy died suddenly on April 28th, 1901.

John Warrington Haward succeeded Pick as Visiting Surgeon to the Atkinson Morley's Convalescent Hospital from 1878–1880. Haward (1841-1921) was born in Essex, a great nephew of Francis Haward RA, the engraver and entered St. George's Medical School in 1860. After qualification he became house surgeon at the Westminster Hospital for a time before returning to St. George's Hospital. Warrington Haward's main interest was in Orthopaedic Surgery and he was appointed Assistant Surgeon to Great Ormond Street in 1870 and to St. George's Hospital in 1875, before becoming Surgeon to the latter in 1880. He was one of the most popular Surgeons who were ever appointed to St. George's and was described as 'a genial conciliatory man, was of the greatest service in soothing over difficulties which otherwise might had been considerable'. Warrington Haward, Treasurer to the Medical School for a number of years was highly regarded in wider medical spheres and became President of the Royal Medical and Chirugical Society. A lover of art and literature, he wrote an excellent series of accounts of the portraits owned by St. George's Hospital. Warrington Haward was one of St. George's greatest servants and everyone was deeply upset when he was forced to resign as a surgeon in 1900 because he had completed his twenty years of service – one of the stupid rules the Board of Governors had introduced and which was currently in force. One of his biographers wrote 'he could take pleasure from contemplating the amount of comfort he had afforded to so many patients through so many years of hard work, and from the fact that he had never been known to shirk his duty on any pretext whatsoever. He never catered for popularity but worked only for two things, the honour and knowledge of his profession.' So St. George's lost one of its finest surgeons and ablest teachers.

During this period the financial plight of the Atkinson Morley's Convalescent Hospital was becoming increasingly precarious, but some slight relief was obtained in 1877 when the Westminster Hospital requested the admission of seven patients and agreed to pay for the necessary nursing staff as well as paying an additional £136-1s-4d to the Management Committee. In the same year a further easing of the situation came about when the Board of Governors decided to sell one acre, three roods and four perches of land for £1,768-7s-8d to avert the financial crisis.

At this time one of the major risks for a hospital inpatient was infectious disease. In 1877 there was one case of smallpox and an outbreak of erysipelas, but thanks to Dr. Poole Collyns, the Resident Medical Officer both outbreaks were contained by isolation. By 1880 it was agreed that children over the age of three could be admitted. Many of the Governors of St. George's Hospital remained boastful of the fact that they had managed to complete the building of the hospital for less than £24,000. Twelve years later it was quite obvious that their cost cutting had only been achieved by scrimping on the quality of the building materials and an acceptance of inferior standards. Some idea of the scale of the disrepair may be gained from a catalogue of the work needed to set matters right. The Chapel ceiling had to be replaced in 1879, and the hospital was forced to close in 1881 because surface water was contaminating the water in the artesian well which supplied the hospital with its domestic water. The problem was rectified by relining the brickwork of the wall with iron cylinders. But a year later the hospital had to close yet again; this time because the drains ceased to function because they had been laid with an inadequate fall, so new drains had to be laid with an increased fall of 1 in 40. Whilst these repairs were taking place the opportunity was taken to whitewash and distemper the internal walls, a sovereign remedy to prevent contagion, and still used to this day in cattle byres.

At the same time as these internal renovations interest was growing in how best to landscape and plant the extensive grounds. Charles Hawkins, the treasurer, gave a number of holly bushes which continue to delight in winter, and Mr. Colebrooke, a Wimbledon resident, presented cedars of Lebanon, fruit trees and many other shrubs. Mr. Colebrooke's Cedars of Lebanon have long been a feature of the grounds of the hospital and survive to this day in the visitor's car park in the front of the hospital, though some sustained damage in the hurricane of 1987. Mr. Colebrooke was a generous supporter of both St. George's and the Atkinson Morley's; and amongst his many gifts was a long case clock which is still in the possession of the parent hospital. Increasingly conscious of the benefits of exercise in convalescence the Management Committee arranged for tar paving to be laid on the south frontage walkway to make it easier for patients to walk outside after heavy rain.

Outbreaks of scarlet fever and smallpox continued to threaten the hospital and in 1884 epidemics occurred which were so severe that the Hospital had to be closed. Both the Wimbledon Local Board and the Kingston Board were asked to take over the infectious patients but they refused, which left the Atkinson Morley's Management Committee feeling very much aggrieved as it took the view that it was entitled to better service in consideration of the extremely high parish rate it paid. Dr. Collyns was again praised for his action in containing the outbreak and he advised the Management Committee that it would be prudent to convert one of the upstairs wards into an isolation ward by the addition of doors and an outside staircase. The Management Committee accepted Dr. Collyns' recommendations and the work was put in hand.

Miss Kyle retired as matron in 1884, and Miss Violet Black took her place. Her immediate task was to supervise an increase in the number of beds from 80 to 90 in 1885, and then to 100 in 1886. Both Miss Kyle and Miss Black were complimented on their control of discipline and expenditure. The average cost per patient was £3-4s in 1886. For reasons that are not clear there was a very rapid turnover of senior staff at the end of this decade. Miss Black resigned as matron after only four years in post and was replaced by Mrs. Tuck. Poole Collyns had proved to be a safe pair of hands in day to day management, as a result he was greatly respected by the Management Committee who had allowed him to assume a wider administrative role than his predecessors so that his duties had grown to be similar to those that the first incumbent, Gregory Smith, had exercised. The Committee had no fears of Poole Collyns exceeding his powers and this trust was well placed. They recorded their sorrow when he tendered his resignation so that he could enter into practice in Wimbledon. Collyns had been an outstanding Medical Officer and Master who was greatly respected by both patients and staff as a doctor and a very able administrator, under whose watchful eye the buildings, the gardens and the grounds at Wimbledon were superbly maintained and developed. One of the Pall Mall Gazette's reporters wrote in the 1930's, 'Not long after it was opened the Convalescent Hospital which is situated in one of the most charming parts of Wimbledon, fell into rather a low financial state, but I believe Mr. R.T. Poole Collyns, who for over twelve years was medical superintendent of the place, brought it back to a very flourishing condition by a wise and economical administration of the funds'. The Governors of St. George's Hospital had previously recognised Collyns' enormous contribution over a period of nearly thirteen years by taking the unprecedented step of electing him as an Honorary Life Governor, an honour he enjoyed until his death in 1906.

After this period of medical stability there was a flurry of activity in both the medical and nursing fields. Mrs Tuck's husband took over the administrative role as Master and Dr. Hugh Lawson was appointed as

Resident Medical Officer. Lawson and the Tucks only stayed in post for one year and then the Management Committee decided to revert to the old system and appointed Dr. H.H. Page as both Master and Resident Medical Officer. Page left after three months and was replaced by retired Brigade Surgeon J.M. Waters of the Army Medical Department. Miss Beachcroft replaced Mrs. Tuck but she resigned within one year and was replaced by Miss Susan Sharp who had previously been Matron's Assistant at St. George's Hospital.

In 1883 William Ewart (1848-1929) took over the medical reins at Atkinson Morley's Convalescent Hospital until 1887. His father was English and mother French, he was educated in England and at the University of Paris before coming to St. George's Hospital Medical School in 1869 where his studies were interrupted for a short period by his participation in the Franco-Prussian war. He qualified in 1873 and the following year obtained the Membership of the Royal College of Physicians before obtaining a house physician post at Addenbrookes Hospital. Whilst at Cambridge he took a Natural Science Tripos from Gonville and Caius in 1876. He passed his Bachelorship in Medicine in 1877, before proceeding to a Doctorate of Medicine and election as a Fellow of the Royal College of Physicians. Ewart was appointed Assistant Physician to St. George's Hospital from 1882 to 1887 and Physician from 1887 to 1907. He was described by Joseph Blomfield, the Anaesthetist, as being indefatigable in the wards and ingenious in devising novel forms of treatment. These, however, were not uniformly successful and since general practitioners of that time gave little encouragement to what was strange to them, his labours in Hospital went unrewarded by a lucrative practice outside it's walls.

The Medical School Gazette of 1929 in an uncharacteristically critical mood, reports that Ewart did not have the qualities that appealed to the public nor was he able to render assistance to family practitioners: 'And thus it came about that William Ewart with great scientific qualities and personal characteristics that endeared him to many, made no headway at all as a Consultant Physician'. William Ewart nevertheless, became legendary for his memorable utterings: when he was looking at a body in the post-mortem room he remarked to the students 'Gentlemen, these are the remains of a patient who is no longer with us'; on another occasion when told of the fate of an unfortunate patient he replied 'Ah poor fellow, death interrupted his recovery'. Ewart was obsessional and loved his work at St. George's being prepared to spend many hours there attending to his patients often to the annoyance of the students who were made to trace the outline of the heart, lungs and liver of patients on tissue paper. As one student said 'the tissue paper used must have filled many a cupboard'. One of his house physicians became so disenchanted by Ewart's interminable ward rounds that he used to despatch one of the students after a couple of hours to the Post Office in Knightsbridge to send a telegram, which he had previously written, to inform himself that he was urgently required elsewhere. It was said of William Ewart that 'No one spent more time or pains in his hospital work' and William Bennett remarked on Ewart's retirement 'What will St. George's do without Dr. Ewart and what will Dr. Ewart do without St. George's.'

The same Bennett responsible for the professional epitaph above was visiting Surgeon to Atkinson Morley's Convalescent Hospital from 1880–1887. William Henry Bennett entered St. George's Hospital in 1869 qualifying in 1873 before becoming a Fellow of the Royal College of Surgeons in 1877. Bennett was appointed 'Chloroformist' to St. George's in 1879 at £20 per annum, having completed House Surgeon and Surgical Registrar posts. He was then appointed Assistant Surgeon in 1880 and Surgeon in 1887, a post he filled until 1905. Bennett was an innovator and thus very quick to recognise the merits of certain advances in practice. He persuaded the Board to buy one of the first cystoscopes, and in 1896 with the advent of radiology he 'desired to bring to the notice of the Board the desirability of occasionally having photographs taken under the new systems for the discovery of certain injuries'. Within two years the Hospital purchased an X-ray machine and appointed a Radiographer.

William Bennett was known as 'the Master' by the students. This was probably a very apt title as Bennett was described as 'a superb surgeon who gained the complete trust and confidence of patients'. The friend of one patient who accompanied her for her consultation with Bennett remarked afterwards 'What a charming man – I must think of some disease to consult him about'. He wrote a chapter on injuries of the spine in Treves' *System of Surgery* and another on concussion of the brain in Allbutt's *System*.

William Bennett was knighted for his services during the South African War and was Chairman to the Star and Garter Homes, St. John's Ambulance Brigade and the Convalescent Homes Committee of the King Edward's Hospital Fund. From his early days he collected porcelain and became a recognised authority on Chinese and English pottery. Students enjoyed his banter with William Ewart. At the bedside of a patient with an undiagnosed complaint Ewart suggested to Bennett, 'Let us go back to Hippocrates'. Bennett replied 'I am unable to take the journey as I have an appointment in a quarter of an hour!'

By 1891 patient numbers had risen to over 1,250 a year and both Miss Sharp and Dr. Waters were praised and given pay rises, the latter's salary was raised from £150 to £200 a year. The Chaplain, the Reverend Marriott, also made a notable contribution to the care of patients and he was given an increase of £50 a year to bring his income up to £150 a year. Waters unfortunately suffered from a long and serious illness the following year so he was not available to deal with the more seriously ill patients who had to be admitted because wards at St. George's had closed for refurbishment. Francis Jaffrey who was later to return as Visiting Surgeon acted as the locum for Dr. Waters.

Serious problems loomed on the horizon as the artesian well required further repairs which were estimated to be very costly. Fortunately the Southwark and Vauxhall Water Company could at last supply water at a pressure sufficient to fill the tank in the tower so the hospital was at last connected to the mains water supply, as a result it was now possible to fit fire hydrants to each floor.

Isambard Owen was the visiting Physician from 1887 to 1893. Sir Isambard Owen was born in 1850 the son of a Great Western Railway engineer, was christened Herbert Isambard but never used his first name, preferring the second which presumably was chosen because of his father's friendship with Isambard Kingdom Brunel (1806-1859) the famous Great Western Railway Engineer. A sprightly man, slight in build with clear blue eyes, Owen was educated in Gloucester before going up to Downing College, Cambridge in 1868 where he wore a beard and was known as 'Goaty'. He entered St. George's Hospital in 1871 and passed his Membership of the Royal College of Surgeons in 1875, Bachelorship of Surgery in 1876, Doctorate of Medicine in 1882 and was elected a Fellow of the Royal College of Physicians in 1885. Now minus the beard but with a nicely trimmed moustache, spruce in appearance and usually wearing a frock coat Owen was elected Assistant Physician in 1883, Physician in 1894 and Consulting Physician in 1905. This long delay in promotion was said to have been caused by William Howship Dickinson, the senior physician who was angry because Owen, when curator, had thrown away a number of Dickinson's favourite specimens. Isambard Owen who was said to have been an excellent host and lover of Sicilian wines became Dean of the Medical School in 1893 and served in this post for ten years. His superb administrative skills and application in promoting the development of sound medical education were rewarded with a succession of glittering appointments: Senior Deputy Chancellor of the University of Wales, Vice-Dean of the Faculty of Medicine, University of London, Principal of Armstrong College, Newcastle and Vice-Chancellor of Bristol University. For these services he was knighted and received a host of honorary degrees. The Medical School Gazette notes the fact that he had a little trait of rolling his 'r's' and most students readily remembered his lecture on the chemical that was used to stuff 'birrrds' and preserve 'furrrrs'. Sir Isambard Owen died in 1926.

Clinton Dent was elected visiting Surgeon from 1887 to 1894. Clinton Thomas Dent, born in 1850 had entered St. George's Hospital Medical School in 1872 from Cambridge. His tenure as Assistant Surgeon for fifteen years (1880-1895) was the longest in the history of the hospital. He ultimately became full Surgeon in 1895, a post he filled until his death in 1912. Clinton Dent was one of St. George's and the Atkinson Morley's greatest servants. He was intensely interested in the welfare of the Hospital, its history and development. Dent was very generous, deeply religious and multi-talented and it was probably because of the diversity of his interests that he failed to gain the recognition which he justly deserved. Dent excelled in everything to which he set his hand. Having served as both Surgeon and War Correspondent in the South African War, he became a Hunterian Professor, a member of the Council of the Royal College of Surgeons and Chief Surgeon to the Metropolitan Police. Short, wiry and bearded Clinton Dent was a brilliant mountaineer and made a number of historic first ascents in the Caucasus before becoming President of the Alpine Club from 1887-1889 and writing his highly acclaimed book 'Above the Skyline'. Clinton Dent was a superb photographer and avid collector of art. Several of his legacies may be seen in St. George's today; these include his commissioned water colour painting by A.D. McCormick of John Hunter's Body leaving St. George's which hangs in the Boardroom, and the stained glass window originally in the chapel at Hyde Park Corner, which is now in the front entrance of Grosvenor Wing. Clinton Dent and Charles Slater were largely responsible for the successful appeal which raised sufficient funds to commission Sir Alfred Gilbert to sculpt the bust of John Hunter to mark the 100th anniversary of his death which now stands in the Medical School Concourse at Tooting.

By the end of the nineteenth century the Atkinson Morley's Hospital was serving as an overspill for St. George's Hospital which was having difficulty in coping with the increasing numbers of patients requiring treatment. The patients now being admitted to Wimbledon were more seriously ill and could no longer be classed as convalescent. In 1894 eight deaths occurred at Wimbledon, the average length of stay was 27 days, and there were 52 male beds and 48 female beds. Shrewd management ensured the hospital finances were in balance. In the Annual Report, Dr. Waters stated that 'the food has been ample in quantity and the quality excellent', 'the cooking has been very good' and 'the vegetable supply from the garden has been abundant'. The patients were clearly enjoying generous quantities of well cooked fresh vegetables but by 1899 his report that 'the vegetable supply not as good owing to scarcity of rain in the summer months' makes dismal reading.

The coach which had carried both patients and laundry between Wimbledon and Hyde Park Corner was showing signs of wear by 1888, despite fairly frequent changes of wheels, and it was therefore decided to purchase a new 'omnibus' from Hurnshaws, the carriage builders of Wimbledon. This vehicle was designed to carry fourteen people, and cost the princely sum of 175 guineas.

Nearly a decade later in 1897 a most unsavoury difficulty arose when the London Sanitary Protection Society discovered that the drains were in such a bad state that the whole system had to be condemned. At the same time the water closets were found to be defective, as a result the hospital was forced to close for 98 days. On a brighter note this brought a financial saving which helped to offset the £2,400 expended on restoring adequate sanitation.

In the last decade of the century, the visiting Physicians were Francis George Penrose, Humphry Rolleston and William Lee Dickinson. Francis George Penrose (1857-1932) was trained at University College Hospital and came to St. George's Hospital in 1888 as Curator of the Museum having first obtained his Doctorate in Medicine and a Fellowship of the Royal College of Physicians. In 1889 he was appointed Assistant Physician to St. George's Hospital and then he gained a similar appointment to the Hospital for Sick Children, Great Ormond Street. He was appointed to the Atkinson Morley's Convalescent Hospital from 1893 to 1896. On Thomas Whipham's retirement in 1897, Penrose was appointed Physician and Lecturer in materia medica, medicine and electricity! His main interests were paediatrics, dermatology, ophthalmology and radiology. It is said that he was a very kind man and very popular amongst the students. In mid-career Penrose suddenly decided to leave St. George's Hospital, at the comparatively early age of 48, to live in Bournemouth where he nursed his sick wife. For the next 27 years until his death he was also able to indulge in his favourite hobby – natural history.

Francis Penrose who served St. George's Hospital from 1889 until 1905 could never have achieved the outstanding success and fame of his successor Dr. Humphry Rolleston. Rolleston (1862-1944) was born in Oxford and educated at Marlborough and St. John's Cambridge, where he gained a first class honours and a 'blue' for rugby football. He entered St. Bartholomew's Hospital as a medical student in 1886 and after qualification he was appointed Curator of the Museum at St. George's Hospital in 1890. Rolleston became Assistant Physician to St. George's Hospital in 1893 and in 1898 he was appointed Physician to both St. George's and the Victoria Hospital for Children. Rolleston was renowned as a physician, pathologist, teacher and researcher, and he gained an international reputation. Honours were heaped on Rolleston from major Universities and Colleges around the world. During the First World War he served as a Surgeon Rear Admiral in the Royal

Navy and for his service he was awarded both the CB and KCB. In 1923 he was appointed physician to King George V, being created first a baronet and then a Knight Grand Cross of the Victorian Order. Sir Humphry Rolleston's presidencies of the Royal Society of Medicine, the Royal College of Physicians, and the Medical Society of London illustrate his pre-eminence in the medical world of his day. Blond and youthful in appearance Rolleston would blush to the roots of his hair if he was embarrassed by a medical student's foolish answer to a question. The reason for this is inexplicable, but needless to say students took every opportunity to exploit this unusual phenomenon. Rolleston served at the Atkinson Morley's Hospital for two years from 1896 when he was replaced by William Lee Dickinson (1862-1904)

William Lee Dickinson was born in London, the son of William Howship Dickinson, a Physician to St. George's Hospital from 1866-1894, and was named Lee after Robert Lee (1793-1877) the first Obstetric Physician to St. George's Hospital for whom his father had a great admiration. William the younger suffered from the grave disadvantage of having to follow in the footsteps of a father who was described by Blomfield 'as a physician who showed unparalleled industry having personality as well as wit and learning who was an effective and popular teacher of students'. Blomfield recalls that Dickinson senior was a large man, silver haired with 'a face, ruddy and often even purpled with suppressed laughter at some unspoken jest. The eyes beneath full eyebrows twinkled blue with humour and intelligence'. He loathed hybrid words and would chuckle derisively at, for example 'parotitis': 'inflammation of the parot indeed'! Dickinson Junior. was educated at Winchester and Gonville and Caius College before entering St. George's Hospital Medical School in 1881. On his father's retirement from St. George's in 1894, he was appointed Assistant Physician. Again following in his father's footsteps he was also appointed Assistant Physician to Great Ormond Street. Poor William Lee Dickinson was faced with a formidable task, as he knew that his achievements would always be measured against those of his father. Undeterred he set out to emulate his father with considerable verve, but unfortunately his hopes of doing so were dashed when his life was cut tragically short. He was unfortunate enough to contract tuberculosis and spent some time in South Africa attempting recovery. Sadly, he suffered a fatal haemoptysis whilst in Cornwall in 1904.

William Lee Dickinson's surgical contemporaries at the Atkinson Morley's Hospital were firstly, and for a short time, George Robertson Turner (1855-1941), then A. Marmaduke Shield (1858-1922) and Francis Jaffrey (1853-1919). George Turner was one of a number of St. George's students who gained International Rugby honours, others included his brother, Edward Beadon Turner, who also became a surgeon, the Tuckers, father and son, J.E.H. Mackinlay, W.E. Collins and H.H. Taylor. George Turner was born in Chigwell, Essex and educated at Uppingham. His family background was strongly medical so it was predictable that he would also follow a career in medicine and he duly entered St. George's Hospital as a student in 1873. George Turner distinguished himself both academically and as a sportsman during his student days, winning a number of prizes including the William Brown exhibition, as well as representing the hospital, the United Hospitals, the South of England, and England, at rugby football. Turner also excelled in other sports including athletics, winning the Inter-Hospitals hurdles in three successive years and coming second in the quarter-mile in 1876. Edward, George's brother had the distinction of playing in both the England twenty and fifteen a side rugby teams despite losing the sight in one eye from diphtheria in 1877. He was also a superb athlete, winning the Inter-Hospitals mile, holding tricycle records for all distances between a half and fifty miles as well as the fifty mile tandem record with S. Lee, an excellent shot and skater as well as holding an extra-masters certificate in navigation. Edward celebrated his 75th birthday by driving from London to Yorkshire at 35mph. After qualifying in 1877, the younger Turner, George, was appointed house surgeon in 1878 and then surgical registrar and anaesthetist in 1880. In 1881 he was appointed surgeon to the Dreadnought Hospital in Greenwich. Six years later he was appointed Assistant Surgeon to St. George's Hospital and elected a full Surgeon in 1887. On the outbreak of war in 1914 Turner was appointed Surgeon Rear Admiral in the Royal Navy serving at Chatham, Plymouth and Malta. He was created a Commander of the Bath in 1917 and in 1919 he received a Knighthood of the British Empire. In his day Turner was a vice-president and honorary secretary of the Medical Society of London; he contributed to a number of books and in addition published a number of papers on the treatment of common surgical conditions. It is remembered that George Turner was 'warm-hearted, breezy, and determined.' Sir Henry Burdett said of him: 'he knows what he wants and usually gets it.' Of himself Turner said 'Democracy makes little appeal to me; I have dared to live without over regard for what people think and say of me.' Turner died in Hove and was buried at Sherbourne Abbey, Dorset.

Turner was followed as Assistant Surgeon to the Atkinson Morley's Hospital in 1898 by Arthur Marmaduke Shield (1858-1922). Marmaduke Shield was born in Laugharne, Carmarthenshire and educated privately before entering St. George's Hospital Medical School in 1875. After qualification he left St. George's Hospital to become in turn Assistant Surgeon to the Westminster Hospital (1886-1887) and Charing Cross Hospital (1887-1893). When a third Assistant Surgical post was created at St. George's Hospital in 1893 Shield who was a bachelor and sported a walrus moustached was appointed, and thus returned to his 'alma mater'. Shield became a full Surgeon in 1900 but his promising career was cut short at the early age of forty nine in 1906 when he was forced to retire after inoculating himself with syphilis whilst operating – a similar fate to that suffered by Herbert William Allingham (1862-1904) a few years earlier. At the time of his retirement Shield also held surgical appointments to the Waterloo Road Hospital for Women and Children, and the Hospital of St. John and St. Elizabeth. During his few years as a surgeon Marmaduke Shield had become widely respected and at times had been Secretary to the Medical Society of London, the Dermatological Society, and the Surgical Section of the British Medical Association, as well as being an examiner at Cambridge and the Apothecaries Hall. It is recorded by Joseph Blomfield that Shield was an 'excellent teacher and full of worldly wisdom'. Gifted with 'a power of admirable mimicry' which 'are supposed not to have increased the appreciation of his seniors'. A 'profoundly witty man' and a gifted raconteur with a fund of stories he was very popular as a teacher amongst the students and much sought after as an after dinner speaker. Shield retired to Budleigh Salterton where he underwent a number of operations on his injured hand and by 1914 his health had improved to such an extent that he returned to surgery and worked throughout the war at a Military Hospital in Exmouth. When the war finished Marmaduke Shield resumed his interrupted retirement, continuing to enjoy his love of the country, golf and fishing. He died whilst on a fishing trip in the Hebrides in 1922.

At the turn of the century the hospital was well established, well regarded and its medical affairs were safe in the capable hands of William Lee Dickinson and Marmaduke Shield, but other aspects were less satisfactory. In addition to Dr Water's *cri de coeur* regarding the paucity of vegetables due to the lack of rain in the growing season, there were anxieties about the effectiveness of the surface drains, but, and more seriously, the hospital's income continued to fall.

It is not difficult to imagine the relief at surviving the nineteenth century with all its vicissitudes, associated with mixed feelings for the future: a sense of trepidation on the one hand and hope for a better and more settled times on the other, which would be felt by those responsible for the Atkinson Morley's Hospital as they entered the twentieth century.

5

Into the Twentieth Century: 1900–1939

The omens were far from good. As if to confirm the worst fears of those whose anxieties centred on the hospital's structure disaster struck almost at once; and the dawn of the new century brought a series of calamities. Tragedy was narrowly averted in October 1901 when the ceilings of the children's ward collapsed. Fortunately, no one was hurt but the architect found that all the ceilings in the hospital were in the same dangerous condition. Many walls needed replastering and the roof required boarding in under the tiles. There was no alternative but to close the Hospital. As early as 1869 several governors of St. George's Hospital were of the opinion that extensive repairs would be required in the future as the contract and specification originally accepted for the building was far too low. Certainly the frequent remedial work of a fundamental nature which had to be undertaken at Wimbledon over the years suggests that the early savings on the building were in the longer term a false economy. Whilst the hospital was closed the opportunity was taken to install electricity; so that the old, inefficient and smelly gas lamps in the wards could be replaced by the relatively recently invented incandescent light bulb.

All the upgrading and refurbishment work together with increases in the cost of salaries, provisions, fuel and rates gave rise to considerable concern over state of the hospital's finances. Expenditure was exceeding income routinely now, and even greater demands were incurred when a new ward boiler and new hot water pipes had to be installed to replace the old ones which had 'furred up' over the years, the porter's lodge was enlarged, and essential repairs had to be carried out in the laundry. The resignation of Dr. Waters added to the pervasive feeling of gloom which was current in the hospital at the time. In recognition of Dr. Waters' outstanding service the Board of Governors awarded him a pension of £120 a year. Dr. William F.C. Dowding replaced Dr. Waters as Resident Medical Officer, but responsibility for the superintendence of the Hospital was handed over to the matron. Dowding, a past Secretary of the St. George's Medical School Club was to serve as Resident Medical Officer at the Atkinson Morley's Hospital for eighteen years – the longest period that anyone held this post.

With the death of William Dickinson in 1904 Cyril Ogle (1861-1931) temporarily took over. Ogle, although a sound and industrious physician who held the office of Censor in the Royal College of Physicians, was a modest and retiring bachelor who never achieved the fame and reputation of his father, John William Ogle (1824-1905) who was Physician to St. George's Hospital from 1857 to 1876.

Soon the highly intellectual yet abrupt, outspoken Arthur Carlyle Latham (1867-1923) was appointed visiting physician to the Atkinson Morley's Hospital. Latham, the son of P.W. Latham, the Downing Professor of Medicine was educated at Fettes, Edinburgh, and Balliol College, Oxford where he obtained a first-class honours in Natural Science in 1892. Qualifying from St. George's in 1894, he continued his medical studies in Vienna, Heidelburg and Berlin before returning to St. George's where he was appointed Assistant Physician in 1898. He shared the Deanship of the Medical School with Francis Jaffrey from 1902 to 1904 and then, in 1905 he became Physician. Latham also held appointments as Physician to the Victoria Hospital for Children, the Brompton Hospital and the Mount Vernon Hospital for Tuberculosis. Latham's reputation lay in his interest in tuberculosis and in 1902 he won a prize with A.W. West, the architect, for an essay on the construction of the proposed King Edward VII Sanatorium at Midhurst. Latham wrote a number of books including one which he edited with Marmaduke Shield, *A System of Treatment*. Arthur Latham took an active part in the foundation of the Royal Society of Medicine in 1907. Latham continued as a Physician to St. George's until 1923, by which time he had antagonised most of his colleagues and patients. A sad ending to the distinguished career of an undoubtedly sensitive and intelligent man who became severely disturbed mentally by a series of personal tragedies.

Latham's co-Dean of the Medical School, Francis Jaffrey (1853-1919) was born in Australia and came to London to work in the City. Disillusioned with the world of high finance he entered St. George's as a medical student in 1882 where he immediately captured the eye of everyone with his prowess on the football field. He became captain of the football team before qualifying in 1887 and after a number of posts around the country he returned as Assistant Surgeon in 1898. Jaffrey was appointed full Surgeon in 1905 and served in this capacity until 1914 when he retired to Fowey in Cornwall. Francis Jaffrey was described as a 'great gentleman, simple in mind who believed the best in everyone and one who never spoke ill of others'. In retirement Jaffrey who was a Fellow of the Zoological Society was able to indulge to the full his deep love for the countryside. He had an accurate and detailed knowledge of it's flora and fauna, and was claimed to know the calls and the eggs of every native bird.

James Stansfield Collier (1870-1935) succeeded Arthur Latham as Visiting Physician to the Atkinson Morley's Hospital. Collier, the son of a Middlesex general practitioner, was educated at the City and Guilds Institute and St. Mary's Hospital. After qualifying in 1894 and holding a number of junior appointments he was elected Assistant Physician to the National Hospital for the Paralysed and Epileptic in 1902 and the following year he was elected to a similar position at St. George's. In 1908 he was elected full physician to St. George's but his election to full Physician to the National Hospital languished in abeyance until 1921. Collier was an eminent member of the Royal College of Physicians and was a Senior Censor. Wearing 'Wimpoles' – black coat and striped trousers, Collier, a brilliant and inspired teacher held the view that overemphasis should not be despised and was said 'to use every histrionic trick of display, eloquence, gesture, and emphasis'. He confessed on one occasion to the Resident Medical Officer, 'Sometimes I am tempted to take liberties with the clinical history and I might be rather embarrassed if

I realised you were listening!.' He was a master of descriptive analogy and exaggeration. Once he described a gouty joint, which had been incised in error as 'pouring buckets of chinese white' and on another occasion when describing the appearance of the brain in a case of syphilitic encephalitis as 'wriggling with spirochetes'. One of his house physicians recalled that at one teaching session Collier showed two patients, one with tabes, the other with disseminated sclerosis, but he demonstrated one as the other and vice-versa, the demonstration was so brilliant that no one spotted the error. It is said 'that no one in the class who saw Dr. Collier lying in carpo-pedal spasm on the table in the large lecture theatre can ever after have failed to recognise the clinical features of tetany'. Undoubtedly, James Collier was an eminent neurologist and contributed to *Brain*, Quain's *Dictionary* and Allbutt and Rolleston's *System of Medicine*; he was much sought after as a lecturer and writer. Collier was a gifted clinician, blessed with a phenomenal memory and a rare diagnostic talent. As a teacher he was described as 'downright, dramatic and inspiring' who attracted large numbers of under- and postgraduates to his teaching sessions at St. George's. Ralph Marnham (1901-1984) who later became a Visiting Surgeon to the Atkinson Morley's recalled that when he was a student on Collier's firm he was reading his notes to the great man on a case of schizophrenia, or dementia praecox as it was known in those days, when he was interrupted 'Much masturbation, Marnham?' Collier asked. 'Yes, Sir,' replied Marnham. 'Ah' Collier said 'Remember, the symptom of many diseases - the cause of none'. And so a popular misconception was rectified. Away from medicine James Collier was acknowledged as an expert fly fisherman, amateur archaeologist and philatelist. After serving as Consulting Physician to St. George's Hospital from 1908 until 1935 James Collier died at his home in Wimpole Street shortly after he retired.

By 1906 Hurnshaw's omnibus was causing problems. It had suffered serious damage in 1893 when it collided with a pole whilst being turned in the grounds of the hospital so the Management Committee agreed that it should be replaced. Messrs. Johnson and Wells of the 'Dog and Fox', Wimbledon High Street offered their coach which the hospital had borrowed on previous occasions but the asking price of £30 was considered to be exorbitant. As motor buses had been introduced into

London a year earlier, it was decided that the hospital should look to motorised transport. In 1908 the hospital occasionally hired a petrol driven omnibus and even went so far as digging an inspection pit in the garage, but it was not until after the beginning of the Great War that a motorised bus was purchased.

Edmund Spriggs (1871-1949) followed James Collier as Visiting Physician in 1907 to Atkinson Morley's Convalescent Hospital. Spriggs, born in Foxton, Leicestershire was educated at Market Harborough Grammar School and Wycliffe College, Stonehouse, before entering a dental practice in Rotherham. At the age of twenty one he obtained a scholarship to Frith College and then entered Guy's Hospital, where he qualified in 1896. He visited Heidelburg in 1901 but returned to England to be elected Assistant Physician to the Royal Hospital for Diseases of the Chest in 1902, to the Victoria Hospital for Children in 1903 and to St. George's Hospital in 1904. Plagued by the debilitating effects of ill-health Spriggs was off for a whole year whist he was Visiting Physician, and his misfortune continued to the point where there was a dramatic reversal in the direction of his career in 1911, when he was forced to resign his positions in London and become Physician to a new sanatorium at Duff Castle, Banff. When this establishment moved to Ruthin Castle, Spriggs followed and remained there for the rest of his life. At Ruthin Spriggs was involved with advances in the treatment of pernicious anaemia with Minot-Murphy. Edmund Spriggs' reputation as a thorough and conscientious clinician with a wide research background ensured that his opinion and services were widely canvassed: as an advisor to the Ministry of Food, as an examiner to the Royal College of Physicians and the University of Aberdeen, and as an inspiring lecturer to medical colleges around the world. Edmund Ivens Spriggs was created a Knight Commander of the Royal Victorian order in 1935. At Ruthin Castle he was very much at home and able to enjoy his favourite pursuits of fishing, golf, tennis, and the breeding and training of golden retrievers, until his death there in 1949.

Herbert Stringfellow 'Pen' Pendlebury (1870-1953) followed Francis Jaffrey as Visiting Surgeon in 1905. He was born in Wigan, the son of a clothing manufacturer, and educated at St. John's College, Grimsargh and Pembroke College, Cambridge where he was a good all-rounder, gaining a First Class Honours in the Natural Science Tripos as well as winning a hockey 'blue' in three successive years. Pendlebury entered St. George's in 1895 and having qualified served in a number of junior posts before becoming an Assistant Surgeon in 1900. In 1906 he was promoted to full Surgeon and obtained similar appointments at the Royal Waterloo Hospital for Women and Children and the Kensington Dispensary and Children's Hospital. Pendlebury was one of the most active protagonists for the amalgamation of the various medical societies to create the Royal Society of Medicine, and when this occurred he became its first Honorary Secretary, later becoming Honorary Treasurer and Honorary Fellow. He also, helped found the Association of Surgeons of Great Britain and Ireland, and was its first Honorary Secretary as well as being on the Council of the Medical Society of London. Pendlebury's son by his first marriage, John, an international high jumper and archaeologist, became British Vice Consul in Crete and was killed during the German invasion in 1942. 'Pen' Pendlebury was described as 'a small, neat, quick, punctual man, successful at all to which he put his hand and an ideal companion'. After retirement from St. George's Pendlebury retired to Malvern where he took an active interest in the College. He died aged 82.

Terence Crisp English (1878-1949) followed Pendlebury as Visiting Surgeon to Atkinson Morley's Convalescent Hospital in 1906. He was the eldest of the five children of Dr. Thomas Johnston English, who originally hailed from the North Riding of Yorkshire, and trained at St. George's to become a South Kensington general practitioner and an anaesthetist to the Cancer Hospital, later to be known as The Royal Marsden Hospital. He was distantly related to another and earlier Terence Crisp English, who had been a pupil under Sir Everard Home, John Hunter's brother in law at St. George's Hospital in 1806. Our Crisp English was educated at Westminster School and St. George's where he qualified in 1900, and took the Fellowship of the Royal College of Surgeons in 1903. On Allingham's sudden death in 1904 Crisp English was elected Assistant Surgeon to St. George's. He was described as 'a sound surgeon of wide interests, and being of handsome appearance and social and intellectual distinction he soon established himself in a very successful practice'. Clearly a surgeon of rare benevolence he was well disposed towards his anaesthetist, for when he was visiting surgeon at Atkinson Morley's he arranged for Mr. Sebastian who had given an anaesthetic to one of his patients to be paid an honorarium of two guineas! Promoted to full Surgeon in 1912, he was commissioned as a Captain in the Royal Army Medical Corps in 1913. During the First World War he served in France, Salonika, and in Northern Italy. Mentioned four times in despatches Crisp English was created Commander of the Order of St. Michael and St. George in 1917 and advanced to Knight Commander of the same order in 1918. Crisp English's other consultant appointments included those at Queen Alexandra's Military Hospital, Millbank, the Royal Hospital, Chelsea, the King Edward VII's Hospital for Officers, the Hospital for St. John and St. Elizabeth, the Royal National Orthopaedic Hospital, the Grosvenor Hospital for Women, Queen Charlotte's Hospital and Beckenham Hospital. He was a very loyal St. George's man and when, in the late 1930s, a number of the medical staff first mooted that the hospital should move out of Central London as an advantageous investment in the future he strongly opposed it. Ivor Back wrote at the time 'St. George stands for England and all that is English. English stood for St. George's and all that is St. George's'. Crisp English had little time for writing, and outside his hospital work his main interests were the British Medical Association and the Goldsmith's Company of which he was Prime Warden in 1937. Crisp English died at his Suffolk country house, Chilton Hall, Sudbury aged 71.

Expenditure rose sharply during the first few years of the twentieth century. In 1908 the hospital was forced to pay its share of the cost of making up Cottenham Park Road, a curious device named 'Wilke's Patent Climax Sliding Partition' was purchased and installed in the Boys' Ward so as to form an isolation cubicle, and iron balconies were fixed to the south side of the hospital. The balconies were completed in the following year when the carbon electric lights were replaced by metal filament lamps which required a voltage of 50 volts instead of the previous 220 volts. This reduction decreased the demand and savings were made in the use of electricity but these modest economies were immediately swallowed up in helping with the cost of replacing fifty bedsteads. Other remedial or new work on the fabric of the buildings continued with new herringbone pattern wood block flooring being laid in the women's' day room and the main dining room. The Manchester Steam Association recommended that the 42 year old boilers needed replacing and Z. D. Berry carried out this work with an enlargement to the boiler house in 1911. Not all was doom and gloom as the hospital received a number of legacies including a very generous one from Mrs. Lilias Marriott, the widow of the late chaplain, and many people donated gifts, such as Mr. W. Ward Cook who gave several games which helped to while away the tedium and were thus much appreciated by the patients.

In 1912 the Medical School after a long hard look, took the Greek adage 'Mens sana in corpora sanate' at it's face value and made an enlightened gesture in deciding to take '14 acres, 1 rood (sic) and 24 poles' of the Atkinson Morley's grounds on an eleven year lease at a rental of £55 a year as a sports ground for the students. Tennis courts, hockey, rugby football and cricket pitches were laid out and a pavilion was built in the south east corner. Over the next 60 years the pavilion had to be replaced on three occasions but the students continued to use the sports grounds until it was decided to move to the London University facilities at Stoke D'Abernon in the 1970's. The playing fields at Wimbledon are still in existence and are presently used by the Old Wimbledonians. In this same year tragedy struck St. George's Hospital Medical School when it lost one of its past students, Edward Wilson (1872-1912) who perished with Captain Robert Falcon Scott RN in the Antarctic on their return from the epic voyage to the South Pole, where they were beaten in their race to be the first party there by Roald Amundsen.

Also in 1912 Walter Fedde Fedden (1878-1952) replaced English as Visiting Surgeon. Fedden had been born in Weston super Mare in Somerset and was a capitation scholar at St. Paul's School before entering St. George's in 1895 where he won several prizes. After the usual house posts at St. George's he was appointed Assistant Surgeon in 1906 barely four years after qualifying in medicine, rising to full Surgeon in 1914 and he held similar appointments at Hampstead General Hospital, the Bolingbroke Hospital and the Victoria Hospital for Children. During the First World War he served for a short period as a Surgeon Lieutenant on HMS China before returning to St. George's where he continued to work until his retirement in 1934. Walter Fedden was described as 'a

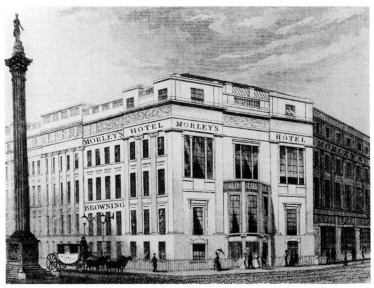

Morley's Hotel – An engraving by John Tallis (*circa* 1845)
Reproduced by kind permission of the Guildhall Library,
Corporation of London

Samuel Armstrong Lane – Surgeon & Owner of 'The School of
Anatomy and Medicine adjoining St. George's Hospital'

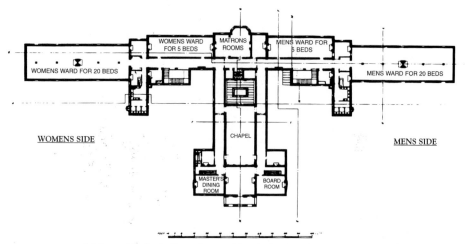

Atkinson Morley's Convalescent Hospital – Ground Floor Layout 1869

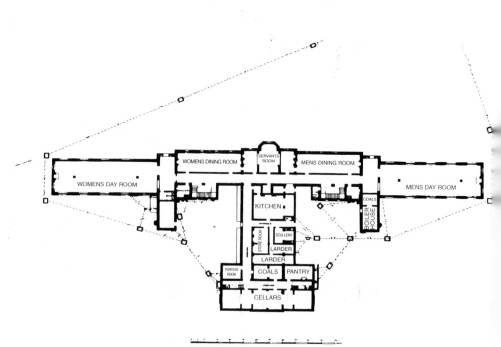

Atkinson Morley's Convalescent Hospital – Basement Layout 1869

Atkinson Morley's Convalescent Hospital (*circa* 1950)

Atkinson Morley's Convalescent Hospital in 1923 showing the newly covered
balconies at rear of building

The Lower Grounds in 1912 just prior to their lease to the Medical School for use as a Sport's Ground

The first Sport's Pavilion opened in 1912

Thomas Tillyer Whipham – Visiting
Physician (1874-1875)

Thomas Pickering Pick – Visiting
Surgeon (1874-1878)

John Warrington Haward – Visiting
Surgeon (1878-1880)

William Ewart – Visiting Physician
(1883-1887)

Arthur Carlyle Latham (on the left)
with Francis Jaffrey – Visiting
Consultants and Co-Deans of the
Medical School (1902-1904)

James Stansfield Collier – Visiting
Physician (1905-1907)

Ivor Gordon Back – Visiting Surgeon
(1914)

Sir Wylie McKissock – Consultant
Neurosurgeon (1942-1971)

Professor Desmond Curran –
Consultant Psychiatrist (1945-1967)

Sir Theodore Crawford – Professor of
Pathology at St. George's Hospital
Medical School (1946-1977)

James Bull – Consultant
Neuroradiologist (1946-1975)

Denis Williams – Consultant
Neurologist (1946-1970)

brilliant anatomist' and 'a loyal friend'. Although he examined for the Universities of Cambridge and London, he wrote little and remains one of St. George's lesser known surgeons but he was said 'to operate with equal skill and facility in every region of the body'. It was also said that he was in 'the first rank as a teacher' and it was recalled by several former students that Fedden's lecture on Venereal Disease was by far the best attended lecture in the school calendar. There was standing room only as he began his lecture with the prophetic words, 'There are only two groups of medical students here, those who have had venereal disease and those who are about to catch it!' The distress and discomfiture of the junior students at their prospects being stated so baldly was always a source of amusement to their seniors. Probably only Kirwan Taylor's lectures in the '40's and '50's on 'L'amour' when he demonstrated the methods of contraception attracted a larger attendance. And neither Fedden's or Kirwan Taylor's lectures were compulsory! Walter Fedden died at his home in Putney aged 73.

Fedden's successor as Visiting Surgeon to the Atkinson Morley's Convalescent Hospital was Ivor Back (1879-1951), who appears to have been arrogant and theatrical by nature, but nevertheless the pampered darling of the highest social strata. Ivor Gordon Back was the eldest son of Francis Formby Back, the proprietor of 'The Egyptian Gazette'. Educated at Marlborough College and Trinity Hall, Cambridge where he was keen on rowing and boxing, he qualified at St. George's in 1905 and became a Fellow of the Royal College of Surgeons two years later. Back was a typical example of the nepotism that was rife at St. George's: after the usual posts within St. George's he was elected Assistant Surgeon within five years of qualifying! During the First World War he served in the Royal Army Medical Corps as a captain at Catterick and in France. In 1918 he was elected full surgeon and worked until his retirement in 1938. The exigencies of wartime lead him to return to St. George's in 1943, and he remained in post until the war was over. He was appointed a Governor of the hospital in 1951 shortly before his death. Ivor Back held other surgical appointments at the Royal Waterloo Hospital for Women and Children, and the Grosvenor Hospital for Women. His special interest was in rectal surgery where he was an acknowledged expert. He was also an examiner for the University of Cambridge, wrote a number of notable papers, and had a large private practice. However, it was outside his professional duties that he became famous. Tall with a striking personality he had a high conceit of himself, and made sure that everyone knew that he was directly descended from the great Duke of Wellington, albeit through his grandmother. As Chairman of the Saville Club he came into contact with many leading personalities of the day and cultivated their friendship. It has been suggested that A.J. Cronin had Back in mind when he was building the character of the surgeon in 'The Citadel'. William Orpen painted Back's portrait, and it will come as no surprise to learn that he appears seated in a white operating gown wearing surgical gloves. The portrait which was first displayed at the Royal Academy Winter Exhibition in 1933, hung for many years in the Saville Club but it was given to St. George's Hospital in 1983 and now hangs in the library. Back held high office in the Grand Lodge of Freemasonry. He was a connoisseur of art and literature and much sought after as an after dinner speaker, but he derived greatest pleasure from acting as an expert medical witness in the courts. He relished the opportunity to put on a polished, theatrical performance and delighted in outwitting both the judge and barristers. In view of this legal connection Back was active in the affairs of the Medical Defence Union and was President in 1949. He died suddenly aged 71 at his home in Connaught Place.

During his time at Atkinson Morley's Convalescent Hospital Back's medical colleague was Arthur John Jex-Blake (1873-1957), who came from a distinguished family of scholars. His father had been headmaster of Rugby before becoming Dean of Wells, one of his sisters was principal of Lady Margaret Hall, Oxford, and the other was Mistress of Girton, Cambridge, and his aunt Sophia was a leader in the campaign to allow women to enter the medical profession. Not to be out-shone by his blue-stockinged relatives Jex-Blake became one of the outstanding physicians at St. George's Hospital, and it was a great pity that he left England at the relatively young age of forty seven to go and live in Kenya with his young wife, Muriel, the daughter of the Earl of Pembroke. Arthur Jex-Blake was educated at Eton before going up to Magdalen College, Oxford, where he took a second class honours in classics before taking a first class honours in chemistry. He entered St. George's in 1897 and during his training excelled both in the lecture hall and on the playing field. He won a number of academic prizes and was a very capable full-back in the school's soccer team. After qualifying he did his house appointments before being awarded a Radcliffe Travelling Fellowship in 1902 and took the opportunity to visit Vienna, Copenhagen and Baltimore. On his return to England he was appointed Assistant Physician to the Victoria Hospital for Children, St. George's and the Brompton Hospital. During the First World War he served as a Major in the Royal Army Medical Corps and how it must have rankled with Ivor Back, that as a surgeon, he was junior in rank to his physician colleague After service in France he returned to St. George's where he was elected Physician in 1919 and seemed to be destined for a place at the top of the profession, but after his marriage in 1920 personal reasons dictated that he should turn his back on what promised to be a glittering career and settle in Africa. It was said of him that he was 'immensely learned in a great variety of subjects, had absolute integrity of purpose and was devoted to the highest ethical standards' and 'a beloved physician'. On the 400th anniversary of the founding of the Royal College of Physicians he wrote a letter in Latin prose on behalf of the sixteen fellows who served in France in the Great War and this letter is preserved in the college library. Arthur Jex-Blake died in Kenya aged 84.

During the First World War the Atkinson Morley's Hospital cared for nearly 1,000 servicemen. The increase in the cost of living during these austerity years caused serious shortfalls in the hospital's budget which was only partly alleviated by War Office grants that in all totalled just over £6,000 for the five year period. When peace was declared, the Atkinson Morley's reverted to its civilian, convalescent role with the long serving Miss Sharp still active as matron. In 1920, after 30 years in post, Miss Sharp resigned, and was replaced by Miss E. Watkins who had previously been matron at the York Road Lying-in Hospital. Mr. Dowding continued in his employment as Resident Medical Officer.

In 1920 there was a deficit in income over expenditure of over £1,200 and the increasing costs of food and coal were plunging the hospital towards financial ruin. In an attempt to stabilise the hospital's finances a contributory payment scheme was introduced where patients were asked to make a payment according to their means. Although about 70% of the patients received free treatment this scheme, along with planned closures for two months in the year (this draconian form of 'financial management' was not new when Kenneth Clark's introduced his Health Service reforms in the 1990s!) and grants from the King Edward's Hospital Fund, helped to bring the income and expenditure almost into balance.

In 1922 the hospital was closed for three months for reasons of economy and James Torrens (1881-1954) and Claude Frankau (1883-1967) were appointed as Visiting Physician and Surgeon respectively. They immediately formed the view that the Hospital was not being fully utilised and recommended that more acute cases should be treated there, and they expressed their opinions with great vigour. The hospital was at this time admitting a number of cases of tuberculosis which lead to the decision to extend and roof over the balconies. Two additional nurses were employed to look after these cases. James Torrens was the grandson of Henry Torrens, the Member of Parliament for Fulham and the son of Henry Torrens who as 'Dana' was Sir Max Beerbohm Tree's business manager. James Torrens was educated at St. Paul's School and St. George's Hospital Medical School where he rowed, played in the three-quarter line and competed in athletics. After a number of junior posts outside of St. George's Torrens returned as Assistant Physician in 1913. During the First World War he served in the Royal Army Medical Corps in France and Mesopotamia. After demobilisation in 1919 he returned to St. George's where he was elected full Physician in 1923. He also held consultant appointments at the Chelsea Hospital for Women, the Harrow Hospital, and the West Middlesex Hospital. James Torrens, who served as Dean of the Medical School, was a good teacher though something of a martinet, who would not tolerate idleness amongst the students. He was a man of mercurial mood swings, sometimes bright and amusing, at other times morose, sarcastic and cynical yet everyone knew that at heart he was full of kindness. Thin and wiry he ate and drank sparingly but had a passionate love for horses and dogs. James Torrens wrote widely and examined for the University, the College, the Apothecaries, and the Conjoint Board. While he was popular in St. George's he failed to achieve the same degree of popularity or distinction as his learned and scholarly successor as Visiting Physician to the Atkinson Morley's, Anthony Feiling.

Anthony Feiling, (1885-1975), came to Atkinson Morley's Convalescent Hospital in 1923. He was named after his uncle, the author Anthony Hope ('The Prisoner of Zenda' etc.) and was educated at Marlborough, Pembroke College, Cambridge, St. Bartholomew's Hospital, and Frankfurt, before serving in the Royal Army Medical Corps in the First World War. He was appointed Assistant Physician to St. George's in 1923 when he relinquished his appointments as physician to the Metropolitan Hospital and the Western Opthalmic Hospital, but retained appointments at the Maida Vale Hospital for Epilepsy and Nervous Diseases and the Royal National Orthopaedic Hospital. Feiling, with distinctive large bushy eyebrows, was precise, well-mannered, elegant, modest, courteous, and gentlemanly. He was elected full physician in 1926 and from then on played a very active part in the development of the hospital and medical school until his retirement in 1950. Although appointed as a general physician Feiling's special interest was in neurology, and he became, in time, both president of the Association of Neurologists, and of the Neurology Section of the Royal Society of Medicine. In addition, he was keenly interested in the affairs of the Royal College of Physicians, where he became a Senior Censor. At St. George's he served as Dean of the Medical School and was highly popular as a teacher amongst the students, mainly for the clarity of his demonstrations and patience in explanation, but also for his gestures and his inability to pronounce his 'r's'. Feiling and his neurological colleague, James Collier were complete opposites. Feiling's careful, precise and accurate lecturing was in direct contrast to Collier's flamboyantly theatrical teaching sessions, during which he would cheerfully bluff his way over any obstacles. Anthony Feiling wrote little and probably because of his great modesty and mild manner he failed to receive the recognition he so richly deserved. Feiling was convinced at an early stage that there was an association between sciatica and lumbar disc protusion, but he failed to publish his observations. He was noted for his generosity to examinees, and it was recalled by Alastair Hunter that on one occasion, after listening to another examiner's condemnation of a candidate to whom he had awarded a zero mark, Feiling remarked that the candidate had done rather well with him and he was awarding him a maximum mark and 'that just lets him go on'. Feiling was one of the consultants at St. George's who later gave their wholehearted support to the establishment of a neurosurgical, neurological and psychiatric unit at the Atkinson Morley's and earlier, as Dean of the Medical School he ensured the appointment of Desmond Curran as the first psychiatrist to St. George's.

During the Second World War Feiling was Sector Hospital Officer in the Emergency Medical Service and after retirement he lived in Le Touquet and the Roding Valley with his wife, Helen who was his cousin, the daughter of Anthony Hope. Still active in mind he died aged 90 and in his obituary it was said of him 'mature when young and young when old'.

Sir Claude Howard Stanley Frankau Kt, DSO, CBE, FRCS, the son of a barrister was educated at Rugby and St. George's. Tall, good looking, serious, and outwardly austere Frankau took his Fellowship of the Royal College of Surgeons in 1908 at the age of 25, one year before he qualified MB BS (a strange reversal of the normal order of events to become a surgeon before he was medically qualified!). In 1912 he was appointed Assistant Surgeon to St. George's. In 1914 he was called up into the Royal Army Medical Corps and served in France where he was rapidly promoted to the rank of Colonel when he became surgeon to the Fifth Army. Three times mentioned in despatches, he was awarded a Distinguished Service Order in 1918 and created a Commander of the British Empire in 1919. On returning to St. George's at the end of the war he took his Mastership in Surgery with a gold medal and in 1926 he was elected a full Surgeon and took charge of the Department of Genito-Urinary Surgery. Later he took over responsibility for the Fracture Department. Claude Frankau had a large private practice and as a consequence he wrote little, but he took an active interest in the Association of Surgeons, and the Section of Surgery of the Royal Society of Medicine, and he became President of both bodies during his career. Frankau also examined for the University, and the College, but it was his administrative skills that serve as his true memorial. Although he took an interest in the development of St. George's, it was his external work that gave him national recognition. During the Second World War he was Director of the Emergency Medical Service for London and the Home Counties – a post of enormous responsibility, as he was the ultimate authority charged with the task of providing medical care and treatment for the many thousands of air-raid casualties. His efficiency was outstanding and he was awarded a Knighthood in 1945. Claude Frankau, a popular member of the Athenaeum Club, married twice; his second wife was Isabella, who was a well known psychiatrist. He died aged 84 at his farm, Ickleton Grange near Saffron Walden where he farmed and bred Jersey cows. In 1925 Frankau resigned as Visiting Surgeon to the Atkinson Morley's Convalescent Hospital to be followed by George Ewart (1886-1942) (see p. 73), Anthony Feiling followed suit a year later and was replaced by Hugh Gainsborough (1893-1980) (see p. 76).

During the 1920s an average of about 1,000 patients per year was treated and this slight fall in numbers was due to an increase in the overall length of stay of the tuberculosis patients, many of whom derived financial support from the London County Council. In addition to the provision of a new boiler, a second lift was installed during this period to assist the movement of bed bound patients around the Hospital.

Towards the end of the decade, the number of patients treated free of charge fell to about 50%, whilst the rest were paid for either by direct contribution, the London County Council approved societies, or by employers. The sale of 'Woodslee' House in Cottenham Park Road for £1,800 and over an acre of land fronting Cottenham Park Road for the building of residential homes for £1,244 brought in funds to ease the financial pressures.

During 1922, W.F.C. Dowding, who had served as Resident Medical Officer for 18 years, retired, and from that time the policy on Resident Medical Officers changed and they were appointed henceforth on short term contracts. The first of whom was Ian S. Thompson, who after a year was replaced by L.M. Jennings, who resigned as Resident Medical Officer in 1925, and A. Harbour was appointed in his stead, but he resigned a year later to be replaced by Mr. C. E. Hagenbach. On the nursing side, Miss E. Watkins was replaced as matron by Miss A.L.M. Rowson, who had been a Sister on Queen Victoria and Rosebery wards at St. George's Hospital; and for the first time a dental surgeon, R. Stephenson was appointed.

One of the most notable events which occurred during this period was the foundation of the Ladies Committee in 1927. This Committee was the forerunner of the League of Friends and its members were meant to act as 'regular visitors to the Hospital' as well as 'co-operating with the management in ensuring the comfort and welfare of patients and staff'. The Ladies Committee very quickly established itself and set about the task of improving the comfort of the hospital for the patients' benefit. Such was its enthusiasm that in its first year the Ladies Committee paid for the decorating and furnishing of the recreation rooms, dining room, and nurses bedrooms, as well as providing 'wireless sets' and gas fires for patients. The ladies also arranged for the removal of the greenhouse from the front of the hospital, the repainting of the garden seats and for apple trees and flowering shrubs to be planted in the grounds. Diverse schemes were employed to raise funds the most lucrative of which proved to be a garden fête.

The fête which was held in 1930 was a grand affair. The band of the Grenadier Guards played throughout the afternoon as those attending could disport themselves by playing in the tennis tournament, visiting the side-shows and stalls, or watching Madame Warlinsy's mannequin parade. Those anxious to peer into their future could have their fortunes told by one of four palmists or clairvoyants. Today the League of Friends continue to give their time generously and work energetically to raise money for the benefit of patients and staff.

In 1928 Dr. T. S. Nelson (1889-1959) replaced Hugh Gainsborough as Visiting Physician. After a brief stay of only a year in post he was followed by C. Blaxland Levick (1896-1953), and at the junior level L. T. Hilliard replaced Hagenbach. Thomas Sidney Nelson was born in Kensington, the son of an engineer. He was educated at King's School, Canterbury, University College, Oxford and St. George's Hospital Medical School. After qualifying he served in the First World War as Medical Officer to the 14th. Brigade, Royal Horse Artillery. After demobilisation he returned to undertake his house officer appointments at St. George's followed by a stint in the post of Assistant Tuberculosis Officer to Bristol. In 1923 he was appointed Assistant Physician to the Brompton Hospital, and in 1926 he obtained a similar appointment to St. George's, and the St. Marylebone Dispensary. By 1935 he had built up a very large and flourishing private practice, when, quite suddenly and to everyone's surprise, he resigned all his appointments to became Consultant Physician to the West Middlesex Hospital, where he set up a medical unit. In 1942 he was enlisted into the Emergency Medical Service and worked at the Upton Hospital, Slough, and the Teddington and Brentford Hospitals. His premature departure from St. George's was greatly regretted as he was considered to be a very good physician. He retired to Haslemere in 1955 where he continued his interests in photography, wood work, and boat building.

Claude Blaxland Levick was born in New South Wales, and completed his medical education in Sydney before he arrived in England soon after graduation. As a student he was a keen lawn tennis and squash player. He worked in Manchester before becoming Resident Medical Officer to the Victoria Hospital for Children, Tite Street, and St. George's Hospital. In 1925 he was appointed Assistant Physician to Tite Street, and to St. George's in 1928. Levick's main interests were in paediatrics and cardiology. The London County Council had established a Rheumatic Clinic at St. George's and it was here that Levick developed his skill in the diagnosis of early heart disease, and these were often reinforced by the use of the electrocardiogram, of which he was an early pioneer. Claude Levick was a great advocate of methodical and careful examination, but he was considered to be a poor formal lecturer, and much preferred the privacy of the bedside to teach his students, with whom he was highly popular. At the outbreak of the Second World War he was at first stationed with the Emergency Medical Service, and then in the Middle East with the Royal Army Medical Corps, where he was mentioned in dispatches, and awarded the OBE. At the end of the war Levick, shy and retiring, but always kind, and of a cherubic appearance, returned to St. George's where he became a full Physician. He was troubled with ill-health, due to hypertension, and he was much mourned when he died at the early age of 57 at his home in Amersham.

The boilers supplying the hospital's heating and domestic hot water were still creating problems in 1930, but F.C. Pay, the engineer to the Savoy Hotel, generously gave his services without charge to survey the existing systems and supervise the installation of new steel boilers, modern piping, calorifiers and radiators. His generosity extended to the donation of the new radiators for the children's ward. At this stage oil supplanted coal as the principal fuel, and at the same time the kitchens were converted to gas. No coal was used in the Hospital henceforth, so the coal cellars could be used for other purposes, which included a dining room for the medical staff.

Miss S. Sharp, the Matron from 1890 to 1920, died in 1931. Miss M.L. Rowley, the senior sister, was promoted to Matron's Assistant in the same year. It was at this time that the Committee of Management recorded that it was 'deeply grateful to the Ladies Committee for the unflagging zeal which it continues to display for the welfare of the patients'. The Committee had provided 'wireless apparatus', gas fires, lockers, chairs and other furniture for the wards. Other gifts included a hut from Dr. Charles Slater, the bacteriologist, which was placed in the garden for children to play in without 'interfering with the comfort of the adults'. Visiting times had been restricted to just Sunday and Thursday afternoons, but now were extended to Tuesday evenings between 5.30 p.m. and 7.00 p.m. so that those visitors who found it inconvenient to visit in the afternoon had an alternative. Even so the Pall Mall Gazette had cause to report 'Wimbledonians themselves know little or nothing about the Convalescent Hospital, which has no other connection with the aristocratic suburb than that it pays it's rates and taxes to the local authorities. A lady who visits regularly among the patients told me yesterday that it is not at all easy to get admission into the wards, and that very strict discipline is kept with regard to the admittance of any outsider, no one being admitted without special permission from headquarters'. Copse Hill was rapidly surrendering it's rustic charms to encroaching suburbia. One of the first intimations of this process is the need to provide adequate access, so the leafy lane was turned into a road. As a result the hospital was forced to sacrifice 12 feet of its frontage which involved the demolition of the wall, the gates, the porters' lodge, and the garage. A new wall and entrance was built and the hospital received over £3,000 in compensation.

Soon afterwards cottages were built beyond the laundry for the resident porter and the laundry engineer close to the boundary fence of Cottenham House which would seem to have been allowed to fall into a state of disrepair as Miss Adele Schuster, who was the occupant, was moved to write to the Governors complaining that she was unable to keep her dogs in, and more importantly the rabbits which had gained access had eaten all her plants and 'left the garden a wilderness'. The House Governor of St. George's was instructed to visit Miss Schuster to explain that the fence was not a high priority! It was during this period that Mr. Read, who had been the laundryman for over forty years, retired, and news reached the hospital of Miss Sharp's death. Both had been devoted servants of the hospital for many years. On Miss Rowson's retirement in 1937, the new matron, Miss Gale, who had been night superintendent at St. George's, acquired the luxury of her own bathroom, which was created by partitioning off part of the boys' ward. Another interesting appointment took place when Horace Williams became Honorary Organist to the hospital chapel. The resident medical officers towards the end of the 1930's included C L Collins, L. Rose, R. Williamson and Geoffrey Theophilus, a St. George's student who gained a blue at Oxford for hockey, and later played at centre-half and captained his country, Wales.

George Ewart handed over the duties of Visiting Surgeon to the handsome George Colquhuon (1888-1951) George Colquhoun was born in London the son of an actuary and educated at Charterhouse, Trinity College, Cambridge, and St. George's. As soon as he qualified in 1914 he joined the army and served in France and Salonika, before being appointed officer in command of the military hospitals at Richborough and Sandwich. After the war he returned to St. George's where he held a number of junior posts before being appointed Assistant Surgeon in 1926 and Surgeon in 1935. Colquhoun suffered from a chronic social disorder that prevented him from taking a sustained interest in the affairs of the hospital, medical school or college, and retired early to his house which was curiously named 'Woodslee' (the name of the house which was in the grounds of the Atkinson Morley's Hospital) in Lymington, and died aged 61 in a nursing home. Colquhoun was replaced as Visiting Surgeon by Bryan Hartop Burns (1897-1985), who was born in Northamptonshire and educated at Wellingborough School, and Clare College, Cambridge. After serving in the Northampton Yeomanry in the 1914-1918 War he completed his medical training at St. George's and in 1926 he was appointed Assistant Surgeon at St. George's, the Belgrave Hospital, and the Royal National Orthopaedic Hospital. He took charge of the orthopaedic department at St. George's and developed the use of plates, the Smith Petersen nail, the Smith Petersen cup and Kuntscher nail which became known as the 'V2' amongst the junior members of the department. This appellation certainly owes more to the nail's shape than the way in which it was inserted! Burns became an examiner for the Royal College of Surgeons, and President of the Orthopaedic Section of the Royal Society of Medicine. During the Second World War he was director of orthopaedic surgery at Botleys Park War Hospital which later became St. Peter's Hospital, Chertsey. After the war he pioneered disc surgery with his colleague Bob Young. Immensely wealthy Burns always seemed slightly remote from his students. During the week he lived in Claridges, and was driven to St. George's by his chauffeur, stopping at the Dorchester for coffee because he felt it was better there than at Claridges. In the out patient department he was quick to admonish patients who smoked but invariably his chauffeur, who wore elegant leather gaiters, was ready to proffer his master a packet of five 'Woodbines' as he left at the end of the session. In the operating theatres he and Young would encourage the registrars who were struggling with the hand driven brace with loud cries of 'Faster, faster!' His large country mansion in Surrey was used by Bob Hope and Bing Crosby when they were making one of the 'Road' pictures. Burns and his wife Dottie were well-known for giving each other extravagant presents, amongst which featured a racehorse and a small West Indian island. Bryan Burns died aged 88.

Bryan Burns was replaced by Marriott Nicholls (1898-1969) as Visiting Surgeon at Atkinson Morley's Convalescent Hospital in 1936. Sir Marriott Fawckner Nicholls was born in London and educated at the City of London School, Clare College, Cambridge, and St. George's Hospital. His undergraduate studies were interrupted by the First World War when he served in the Royal Fusiliers from 1915 to 1919 and was demobilised with the rank of Captain. After qualification he served in a number of junior posts including that of curator to the museum. In later life he never seemed to be happier than when he was sitting in the pathology museum demonstrating the specimens as he lectured to his students – he was a first class teacher, an outstanding clinician, and brilliant administrator. He was appointed Assistant Surgeon to

St. George's in 1932 and Surgeon in 1936 and also held similar appointments to the Royal National Orthopaedic Hospital, The Royal Chest, and the Belgrave Children's Hospitals. His main interest was in genito-urinary surgery, and he was at various times on the council of the Association of Urological Surgeons, and President of the Section of Urology of the Royal Society of Medicine. 'Nick' as he was affectionately known became Dean of the Medical School in 1936 and served in this post until 1956, although he was away in the RAMC from 1940-1946. During this period he served as a Lieutenant Colonel in Freetown, and later as a Brigadier to the 14th Army, South East Asia Command. He was appointed CBE in 1946. On his return to St. George's as Dean he was faced with difficulties arising from the uncertainty as to the future location of the expanding hospital and medical school. A new site had been identified in Tooting but it was geographically far removed from Hyde Park Corner (not the least fault among many others, some critics were to mutter), and presented problems with regard to accommodation and transport for the students and teachers. With tact and steady diplomacy he overcame these difficulties and St. George's has good reason to be grateful to Marriott Nicholls' skill as an administrator. Nicholls was the first to move his clinical department to Tooting to demonstrate his decisive leadership, but it was the great respect, trust, and esteem in which he was held by his colleagues that overcame difficulties as they arose. Nicholls was one of the visionary leaders who pursued a policy of academic development in the school, and he was the driving force behind the gradual evolution of a series of new university departments and their academic staffs. Undoubtedly 'Nick' was one of the greatest deans in the history of St. George's and it was a sad day when his beloved Lagonda was no longer seen on the forecourt outside of the school at Hyde Park Corner. In 1956 he relinquished the post of Dean, but with undiminished zeal it was only natural that he should turn his attention to establishing a Department of Academic Surgery, so by the time he took retirement at the age of 64, its foundation was recognised by the University and a chair in surgery had been established. After his retirement Marriott Nicholls became Professor of Surgery in the University of Khartoum, where he was held in the same warmth and high regard that he had been at St. George's. For his work there he was awarded a KBE in 1969. Nicholls was a tall man of distinguished military appearance who could appear to be aloof but in fact was one of the most approachable of men and was held in the greatest of respect by all who worked with him. He had a love for cricket and fishing, and he was a staunch supporter of the school cricket club, and often turned out for the team when it played on tour in Northleach where he had a home. 'Nick' was noted for his genial hospitality. He died in Khartoum aged 71.

6

The Second World War:
A Period of Change:
1939–1945

By 1939 the number of beds at Atkinson Morley's Convalescent Hospital had been reduced to 74 in an attempt to cut costs but even this reduction could not prevent the accumulating deficit. However, a new role could be seen for the hospital as plans were drawn up to rebuild St. George's Hospital at Hyde Park Corner. Mr. Percy William Adams, the hospital architect, was instructed to draw up plans for the Atkinson Morley to house 110 beds, with full ancillary services, so that it could be used to complement and relieve beds at Hyde Park Corner. Adams completed his plans which would have cost £15,000 to execute but the plan had to be abandoned, when the storm clouds of war gathered across Europe, and instead planning was restricted to the provision of two air-raid shelters with full black-out protection in the basement of the hospital. At the same time a static water tank was sited in the grounds in case of bomb damage to the water main. It was also decided by the Board of Governors that, with the threat of bombing raids on central London, the Preliminary Training School for Nurses should be transferred to Wimbledon, where suitable dormitories and lecture theatre facilities would have to be provided.

As soon as war was declared Nicholls enlisted and handed over the post of Visiting Surgeon to the Atkinson Morley's Hospital to Ralph Marnham (1901-1984). Sir Ralph Marnham was the twelfth of the general surgeons of St. George's Hospital to become Sergeant Surgeon to a reigning monarch but the only one to achieve the honour in this century. Ralph (pronounced Rayf) was born in Stellenbosch, South Africa in 1901 and educated at the Diocesan College, Rondebosch, Gonville and Caius College, Cambridge, and St. George's Hospital, where he rowed, played rugby football, and golf in which he achieved a handicap of eight. In 1934, he was elected Assistant Surgeon but soon after the beginning of the Second World War, Marnham relinquished the post of Visiting Surgeon to the Atkinson Morley's Hospital and joined the RAMC as a surgical specialist. It is told that Marnham spent the first few months of the war as Chief Surgeon at what had become known as the Casualty Clearing Station at Hyde Park Corner, but on seeing Desmond Curran in a Surgeon Captain's uniform he became so enraged that he appealed to Sir Claude Frankau, who was the sector officer of the Emergency Medical Services, to be transferred into the Army proper.

In the RAMC, Marnham was promoted to Brigadier, and became Surgeon to the 9th Army and was twice mentioned in despatches. On demobilisation in 1945 he returned to St. George's Hospital as a Consultant Surgeon and was also appointed to the surgical staff, King Edward VII Hospital, Mount Vernon Hospital, and the Royal Canadian War Memorial Hospital at Taplow. In 1946, Ralph Marnham became Surgeon to the Royal household of King George VI. Later, he was appointed Surgeon to Queen Elizabeth II, and then Sergeant Surgeon from 1967 to 1971. Marnham was created a KCVO in 1957.

Marnham published very little but will be remembered as a very quiet, dextrous, and safe surgeon, an excellent teacher who was justifiably popular with colleagues, theatre staff and students and an excellent all-round doctor who was kind and gentle to his patients. He had a large and successful private practice; as a consequence he was always in a hurry. On rushing out of the Outpatients Department on one occasion he turned to his house surgeon and said 'stick close to me m'boy – I lost many a house surgeon between here and the wards!' He never changed in theatre, he would only remove his shirt and tie, and operated in his vest. Sir Ralph was President of the Association of Surgeons of Great Britain and Ireland in 1965, and President of the Medical Defence Union from 1970 to 1976.

As soon as Marnham joined the army in 1940, Victor Riddell (1905-1976) became Visiting Surgeon to the Atkinson Morley's. Born into a medical family, the young Riddell burdened with the forenames of Victor Horsley, after the renowned neurosurgeon, could be destined only for a career in medicine. He was educated at Clifton, Cambridge, and St. George's Hospital. As an undergraduate Riddell kept wicket in the Varsity match. After obtaining his fellowship in 1933 he undertook a number of junior surgical appointments at St. George's including that of Resident Surgical Officer when he became one of the early pioneers of blood transfusion. If a transfusion was going to be necessary in those early days, the patient's relatives were called to the hospital, their blood was crudely grouped, and those whose blood most nearly matched that of the patient were bled in the casualty department. The blood was then give to the patient by injection through a three way syringe where it could be mixed with an equal volume of saline solution. The process was laborious and often took a whole afternoon. Later Riddell introduced an electrically driven rotary pump to administer the blood. The pump had two speeds which Riddell with his typical grandiloquence named 'petite vitesse' and 'grande vitesse'.

Victor Riddell was appointed Assistant Surgeon in 1939 and remained at St. George's throughout the war, where he attended many of the casualties from the bombing raids. Riddell was appointed a full Surgeon in 1946 and served St. George's until his retirement in 1970. His main surgical interests were breast and thyroid surgery, in which he was one of the first to advocate routine identification of the recurrent laryngeal nerve. Victor Riddell's surgery was always precise, immaculate, gentle and bloodless, but as the years passed he became increasingly pompous and distanced himself from his colleagues and friends. In his early years he was happy to pronounce his name as *'Riddle'* but later when he felt a knighthood was in the offing he sent round a memo informing everyone that he wished to be called Mr Victor *'Rid-dell'* in the future.

Claude Levick also volunteered for military service in 1940 and was replaced as Visiting Physician by E. Bellingham-Smith (1881-1970) Eric Bellingham-Smith, born in Lee, Kent received his medical education at

Guy's, where his brother, who was also a well known artist, was an obstetrician and gynaecologist. After qualification Bellingham-Smith was at first tempted to follow in the footsteps of his brother but very soon decided to specialise in general medicine and paediatrics and began working at the Queen's Hospital for Children which later became known as the Queen Elizabeth Hospital. During the First World War he worked in Serbia for a brief period before joining the RAMC and serving in Egypt.

Bellingham-Smith was appointed Assistant Physician to St. George's in 1920 and in 1923 was promoted to full Physician, a post he held until his retirement in 1946. After he retired he moved to Sussex but kept in frequent touch with his friend and colleague, Anthony Feiling with whom he wrote a *Textbook of Modern Medical Treatment*. Eric Bellingham-Smith is remembered as a fine physician, a meticulous teacher, a loveable character, and a humble Christian gentleman. He must also have been a tough and resilient character, as he suffered a serious illness, and underwent a major operation in 1941, yet despite a chronic disability he survived and was active for another twenty nine years.

In 1940 the Atkinson Morley's Hospital experienced the effects of the German air raids when some high explosive bombs were dropped in very close proximity. Fortunately the hospital suffered no real harm apart from minor damage to the roof, windows, and the patio which cost £510 to repair. Just before Christmas that year a large number of incendiary bombs were dropped in the grounds but again luckily none fell on the hospital. Wartime Britain was subjected to severe rationing and households were encouraged to 'Dig for Victory' in order to grow their own vegetables and fruits. The Surrey County War Agricultural Executive Committee decreed that two and a half acres of the hospital land south of the laundry should be cultivated and used to grow vegetables. The hospital management committee found that they had insufficient manpower to carry out such an order, so, for the duration of the war, the land was handed over to the Borough of Wimbledon, and was divided into allotments for the use of Wimbledon and Merton residents.

As central London became increasingly subject to attack from the air, the Ministry of Health asked the Board of Governors of St. George's

Hospital if it could carry on some of its work outside London. The Berkshire County Council suggested that Windsor Emergency Hospital could be used for this purpose. The Governors and medical staff decided that such a transfer would be difficult to arrange, so they suggested to the Ministry that the Atkinson Morley's Hospital should be adapted to deal with general acute work. The Minister of Health readily gave his approval and arrangements were immediately put in hand to upgrade the Atkinson Morley's with the object of increasing its bed complement to 120. Arrangements were also made to include an operating theatre, a radiology department, and sanitary tower within the upgrading scheme. It was hoped that the alterations and additions could be completed by May 1942 at a total cost of £4,500. The Ministry of Health later insisted that the roof and windows should be strengthened to meet air raid precautionary standards, and the Ministry agreed to donate £582 towards the costs.

The Board purchased a new x-ray machine costing £2,400 for the Atkinson Morley's Hospital in 1942. This was a very generous gesture as St. George's Hospital was having to make do with a machine that had been purchased in 1927 and after fifteen years of constant use was of a temperamental disposition, so that on occasions patients were forced to go to the senior radiologist's, Dr. Mather Cordiner's, private rooms in Harley Street for x-ray examination.

With the additional staff needed to cope with the proposed increases in the workload of the hospital, and the transfer of the nurses' preliminary training school from Hyde Park Corner, an expansion of the residential accommodation was urgently required. Fortunately, Possil House standing in three acres of grounds, and just one hundred yards up Copse Hill from the hospital, at 23 Copse Hill was available for purchase. Possil House was purchased from Sir Harry Twyford, the Lord Mayor of London, for £9,000 by St. George's in 1941. The building had originally been called Ormond House, but this was changed to Possil in 1913 by the then owner Sir Archibald Alison, who had a house in Devon which he also called Possil after the name of his grandfather's house in Glasgow. Possil House which had been built in the 1850's was large enough to accommodate nearly sixty nurses, and, with its extensive grounds, it proved to be a valuable acquisition. The hospital took on Sir

Harry's gardener, a Mr. Green, at a salary of £3 per week plus a cottage at the back of Atkinson Morley's with free electricity and two tons of coal a year in the hope that he would provide sufficient vegetables for both patients and staff at both hospitals from Possil's kitchen garden!

At the end of 1941 Dr. George Theophilus resigned as RMO and Dr. F. Seaton Winton replaced him as the work continued which would change the remit of the Atkinson Morley's from a strictly convalescent facility into a predominantly acute hospital, but the financial deficit for the year stood at £1,348 – the largest in the hospital's history to date, and especially alarming when just over 600 patients were admitted and little maintenance had been carried out.

At the beginning of 1942 the Governors also took a lease on Cottenham House which stood just to the north of the hospital grounds on the Cottenham Park Estate. It had been built for George Walker, a former Ridgeway resident on the old Prospect Place site in 1869. Although it was in a poor state of repair, the house with its listed coach house and stables was to serve the hospital well for a number of purposes in the coming years. Interestingly, under the house are a number of cellars linked to underground passages which run for substantial distances through the hospital grounds. These passages were probably built for the original Prospect Place and were most likely used for cold storage. They have now been sealed off. The property was eventually purchased in 1950 for £9,850. Once the Governors had signed the lease, Cottenham House was sub-let to the Medical School for £350 a year for use as bacteriology, pathology and bio-chemical laboratories. The hospital agreed to bear 75% of the cost of furnishing and equipping the laboratories. Later the house was used for residential and other purposes.

By the autumn of 1942 the Atkinson Morley's was at last ready to accept acute surgical and medical admissions. The hospital governors appointed Mr. G.A. Ewart (1886-1942) and Dr. E. Bellingham-Smith as the Consultant Surgeon and Consultant Physician responsible for the acute surgical and medical beds at the Atkinson Morley's Hospital. Thus the usage of the hospital according to Atkinson Morley's wishes had been altered irrevocably, and within a relatively short period of time his original intentions would be consigned to history. However the change, when it arrived, would prove to be much greater than anyone had envisaged, and a combination of misfortune and serendipity played a major role in determining the future of the Atkinson Morley's Hospital.

George Arthur Ewart was the son of James Cossar Ewart MD FRS, the Regius Professor of Natural History in Edinburgh and Sophia, the sister of Sir George Turner, who had been Visiting Surgeon to the Atkinson Morley's at the end of the nineteenth century. Ewart was educated at the Edinburgh Academy, Clifton College, Edinburgh University, and Christ's College, Cambridge, where he won a 'blue' as a cross country runner. He entered St. George's in 1909 and was elected Assistant Surgeon in 1914, the year in which he also married Dorothy, his first cousin and the younger daughter of Sir George Turner. Ewart was also elected to similar surgical appointments at the Hospital for St. John and St. Elizabeth and the Rupture Society. After serving as a major with the RAMC in France during the Great War he returned to St. George's and was elected full Surgeon in 1932. Ewart of rugged country appearance enjoyed shooting, photography, natural history and socialising. Desmond Curran in commenting on some of his contemporaries noted Ewart's fondness for drink in convivial company. He was a good teacher but a rather histrionic surgeon who enjoyed the drama of the operating theatre, particularly emergency operations; so it perhaps came as something of a surprise to find that he was entrusted with the task of establishing elective general surgery at the Atkinson Morley's. At this point fate took a hand, and in October 1942, two weeks before he was due to start work at the hospital he suffered a fatal coronary thrombosis at his home in Weybridge at the age of 56. George Ewart's son, Gavin (1916-1995), was tipped as a potential successor to John Betjeman as Poet Laureate, but despite writing some verses to mark the birth of Prince Harry he failed to be appointed, possibly because some other examples of his work were regarded as facile.

At the same time our Canadian allies, who had by now entered the war, were searching for an emergency hospital, and the Ministry of Health agreed that Leavesden Emergency Hospital should be handed over to the 10th Canadian Hospital Unit. Leavesden at that time housed an efficient and industrious emergency head injury unit which was under the charge of Wylie McKissock. This edict appeared to deal a mortal blow to the fledgling unit, but out of unsettled circumstances may occur opportunities as well as disasters, and this apparently harsh and distant decision lead indirectly to major, if unforeseen, repercussions for the future direction in which the Atkinson Morley's Hospital was to move. Wylie McKissock (1906-1994), the son of a chemist born in Staines, Middlesex had been educated at the City of London School, King's College, London, and St. George's Hospital. On qualifying in 1930, he passed his fellowship two years later and was appointed a surgical registrar at St. George's. Prizes came his way and promotion to Resident Surgical Officer was rapid, which made others jealous of his drive, determination and ability, and no doubt they felt threatened by his intense dislike of incompetence, his inability to suffer fools gladly, as well as his profound mistrust of officialdom. His career received a temporary setback when, while still the RSO, he had the temerity to get married and found on his return from honeymoon that he had been ousted from his post. It was all too obvious that his enemies at St. George's were determined to stop him from becoming a Consultant Surgeon at the hospital at any cost. Little did they appreciate Wylie's tenacious character or foresee that he would eventually turn the tables on them. Wylie secured a post as a neurosurgical registrar at the Maida Vale Hospital for Nervous Diseases where he worked under Charles Donald. After a short spell at the Hospital for Sick Children, Great Ormond Street, he succeeded Donald as Neurological Surgeon to Maida Vale in 1936. Wylie McKissock then travelled on a Rockefeller Fellowship to the Lahey Clinic in Boston, Massachusetts where he saw the neurosurgical developments of the New World at first hand, and wrote to his new wife a series of engaging pen-portraits describing what he thought of it all. In 1937 McKissock travelled to Stockholm where he spent some time studying with Herbert Olivecrona, then Europe's most renowned neurosurgeon. It was here that he met and observed Eric Lysolm, the father of neuroradiology who influenced McKissock's thinking dramatically. Wylie recognised the paramount importance of radiology in the diagnosis and treatment of brain disease and trauma. McKissock returned to England and with others developed ventriculography and lumbar air encephalography. Later in his career he was to encourage the development of arteriography, ultrasonic scanning, and saw the enormous potential of the non-invasive techniques of computerised tomography and magnetic resonance imaging.

By 1939 McKissock was appointed consultant neurological surgeon to the Hospital for Sick Children and associate neurological surgeon to St. George's. On the outbreak of war McKissock was rejected by the army as being medically unfit for active service, but given the opportunity to establish and take charge of the Head Injury Centre at Leavesden Emergency Hospital. In early 1940 he was appointed honorary neurological surgeon to the Burden Neurological Institute in Bristol. The Ministry's decision to hand Leavesden over to the Canadians came as a bomb shell to McKissock as it looked as though his unit would be shortly dismantled. Wylie McKissock was determined to find other accommodation so he turned to his old teaching hospital where the Governors were now facing a quandary as to how best to plug the gap left at Wimbledon caused by Ewart's unexpected demise. McKissock saved St. George's and St. George's saved McKissock. The Board agreed with alacrity to McKissock's request that he should take over the surgical wards at the Atkinson Morley's Hospital for neurosurgery. Thus the Neurosurgical unit with sixty beds came into being under McKissock's care in November 1942, with Valentine Logue, another St. George's man, as his assistant; two resident house officer completed the medical establishment. Fortunately, the Board of Governors had already made sound arrangements for the opening of surgical and medical wards at the Atkinson Morley's Hospital so the sudden switch to Neurosurgery did not present insuperable obstacles. Dr. Hugh Gainsborough, the Physician at St. George's Hospital, was posted by the Ministry of Health as medical officer in charge, Victor Riddell resigned as Visiting Surgeon, and both Dr. Bellingham-Smith's and Dr. Seaton Winton's appointments were terminated. The Reverend Cowley resigned and Canon A.H. Phelps, the vicar of Wimbledon, assumed the chaplaincy; although it is hard to see any connection between this and the other staff changes taking place at that time.

The total cost of the upgrading amounted to £6,391. The hospital was now no longer called the Atkinson Morley's Convalescent Hospital, but the Atkinson Morley's Emergency Hospital. It would not be too long before it became known simply as the Atkinson Morley's Hospital, and later this in turn was abbreviated by the majority of patients and staff to AMH, which marked the great affection in which the hospital was held by all.

Hugh Gainsborough was born in Leeds of Russian and Dutch Jewish parentage and educated at Downing College, Cambridge, and St. George's. After qualification in 1917 he served as a captain in the RAMC in both India and Mesopotamia before returning to St. George's where he was made an Assistant Physician in 1926, and Physician in 1928. 'Papa' Gainsborough as he was known, was to the average student a poor teacher and a worse lecturer, but few would deny his competence and honesty as a clinician, his concern for patients, and his outstanding ability as a scientist: in conjunction with John Addy Gardner he produced important papers on diabetes, renal disease and steroid metabolism. Long before the introduction of endoscopy into clinical practice he was one of the first to advocate the importance of its development. Of 'leftish' and slightly paranoid views, which were more often than not at variance with those of his colleagues, and his strong, yet occasionally unjustified, support of the 'underdog', Gainsborough disliked private practice and enthusiastically embraced the concept for the rebuilding of St. George's in a populous suburb, with the synchronous development of clinical academic departments staffed by whole time salaried clinicians. His appointment to the Atkinson Morley's Hospital as the Medical Officer in Charge presented him with the ideal opportunity to establish a twenty bedded gastro-enterological clinical academic unit.

Gainsborough soon turned his attention to psychosomatic medicine in which he collaborated with Elliot Slater, and his friend, Emanuel Miller, (father of Dr Jonathan Miller who, after qualifying, briefly followed a career in psychiatry and neurology before turning to the stage and becoming well-known for his contribution to 'Beyond the Fringe', and even more famous for his subsequent theatrical and operatic productions) on a survey of psychological factors in gastro-intestinal disease which soon seemed to render him even less decisive than previously. Gainsborough was the complete antithesis of McKissock, and their units rubbed along in uneasy coexistence until the end of the war, when Gainsborough returned to Hyde Park Corner. In 1957 he became the Director of the newly established Medical Unit, which on his retirement in 1959 became a Professorial department. Gainsborough together with his brother, John, an architect, influenced the architectural design of the present St. George's at Tooting. Desmond Curran later referred to Gainsborough as 'that failed planner'.

In addition to McKissock's 60 beds and Gainsborough's 20 beds, the hospital held ten beds reserved for the emergency medical service, and 40 beds were earmarked for convalescent patients. At this time the local management committee was disbanded and the hospital was brought under the direct control of the House Committee of St. George's Hospital.

The seven sisters, the forty three nurses and the ten maids who were required to look after these acutely ill patients were accommodated at the newly acquired No. 2 The Drive, Possil House and on the upper floor of the hospital itself. The kitchen garden at Possil more than fulfilled expectations, and Mr. Green was complimented on growing sufficient vegetables to fully supply both the town and country branch of St. George's.

The rapid growth and development of Atkinson Morley's Hospital was now well underway. St. Theresa's Hospital in The Downs which belonged to the St. Anne Order of Sisters, placed twelve beds at the disposal of the Atkinson Morley's Hospital in 1943. These beds were initially mainly for children but later these became adult beds and this arrangement remained until St. Theresa's closed in 1986.

It did not take the Governors long to recognise the value of a neurosurgical unit, and the desirability of retaining it after the war ended. Quickly they took steps to achieve this by appointing Wylie McKissock as Consultant Neurological Surgeon to St. George's Hospital in 1944. The Neurosurgical Unit was now secure within the St. George's ambit although it did transfer for five months after D-Day, to the Royal United Hospital, Bath, to deal with casualties from the second front. In a last desperate attempt to win the war, Adolf Hitler unleashed his deadly V1 and V2 weapons on London in late 1944 and a V1 flying bomb exploded close to the Atkinson Morley's Hospital but luckily only damaged a few windows. The sports pavilion was destroyed at about this time by an accidental civilian fire, to overcome this deficiency a part of Cottenham House was partitioned off and used as a temporary pavilion. With the advent of peace in 1945, some consultants at St. George's favoured the Atkinson Morley's Hospital reverting to a convalescent facility once more, but Wylie McKissock had other ideas.

7

The Development of a Centre for Neurosciences

Almost immediately after Wylie McKissock was given the opportunity to establish his emergency unit at the Atkinson Morley's Hospital he began to embark on his overarching ambition to develop his department and, in doing so, establish the Hospital as a major Neuroscience Centre. It is doubtful whether anyone but McKissock would have possessed the determination and drive to engineer these changes and achieve his aims in so short a time. McKissock believed that the ideal unit, one which would scale the heights and gain international recognition, should include not only neurosurgery and neurology, but psychiatry, as well as highly specialised support units such as radiology, anaesthetics, medical physics, and last, but not least, rehabilitation.

As soon as the war was over and Hugh Gainsborough had returned to Hyde Park Corner, McKissock invited the recently demobilised Desmond Curran (1903-1985), the psychiatrist, and James Bull (1911-1987) the radiologist, to join him at the AMH to develop their own specialised departments. Later the newly appointed neurologist to St. George's, Denis Williams (1908-1990) was invited to have his inpatient beds at Wimbledon. McKissock now had his 'core team' which would help him to establish the international status of AMH in the treatment of neurological and psychiatric disorders.

McKissock and the others were very fortunate to have the help of a most capable and far-sighted Hospital Secretary, Robert Fairweather. Fairweather had started his career as an Administrative Assistant at St. George's Hospital prior to 1939. During the war he joined the Army, reaching the rank of major, and winning the Military Cross whilst serving in the desert. On demobilisation, he was sent by Philip Constable, the House Governor at St. George's, to Wimbledon to help McKissock.

Bob Fairweather was to McKissock the ideal administrator, a decisive man who was prepared to slash through 'red tape' when it interfered with progress, and whose aim was to complete a task as quickly and as efficiently as possible causing minimal disturbance in the process. In short he was that extremely rare bird in management: a facilitator rather than an inhibitor. The two held one another in great mutual regard, and together made an irresistible team, so that between them they skilfully engineered the necessary structural and staffing changes required to establish the new departments and facilities. All these developments were taking place simultaneously against the background of a much more profound philosophical change in the provision of health care: from the comparative cosiness and independence of being part of a voluntary hospital, to being taken under state control through its National Health Service which was introduced in 1948. It was McKissock's great good fortune that right up to the time he retired in 1971, St. George's retained its own Board of Governors, of which he was a member for many years. As a teaching hospital it's Board enjoyed a degree of autonomy denied to the vast majority of hospitals, but in addition it also had important and influential direct links with the Department of Health. All of these factors helped Wylie McKissock to bring about definitive changes rapidly, which would have been impossible for him to have accomplished in more recent times after the dissolution of the Board of Governors and the formation of Health Authorities. 'Cometh the hour, cometh the man'. One may only speculate as to quite how he would have fared in these days following the introduction of trusts and purchasing authorities, but it is safe to say that he would have found them an anathema to work with, and his creative genius would have been blunted by the endless frustrations engendered by the current management structures.

The neurosurgical wards occupied the old large male and female convalescent wards on the ground floor, and with the installation of the new regime, the nursing staff had to adapt quickly to the way McKissock wished his patients to be looked after. Many weird and wonderful stories began to filter back to Hyde Park Corner regarding the peculiarities of patient care which were being introduced at Wimbledon. Quarter hourly observations of basic parameters (pulse and blood pressure) seemed bizarre until the need for these were appreciated. The position of the beds was reversed, with the head of the patient orientated towards the centre of the ward, which allowed the operative incisions to be inspected and dressed with the minimum of disturbance to the patient and the maximum amount of space available to the dresser, who was always a Registrar. Silver foil was placed directly over the wounds to prevent the dressings adhering to the wound, and to prevent infection, traffic in and out of the ward was curtailed by locking the doors between 10 am and noon whilst dressings were being carried out. Many young Registrars found it difficult to apply the head dressings initially as the nurses were not supposed to help hold the head, and the standard package of materials seemed to be never-ending with layer after layer of gauze swabs being ever more precariously applied; the sense of achievement at having wound the crepe bandage round the patient's head and clipped home the seventh and final safety pin (yes – always seven!) tucking the edge surrounding the patient's face under the rest of the dressing, was enormous. Gradually the finished product grew less like a Papal tiara worn at a rakish angle and more like a snugly fitting crash helmet.

Soon student nurses began to look forward to their time at Wimbledon, particularly when they began to realise their observations of minute alterations in the patients' condition were of crucial importance, and could spell the difference between life and death if they were conveyed quickly enough to the doctors. This level of responsibility was a new dimension for most of them, it was 'real nursing', and they were made to feel an integral part of the team. It was hard to find anyone who had not enjoyed their stay at the hospital, and a large number returned to more senior posts on qualification. Some nurses confessed to the fear that remote Wimbledon would not offer them the breadth and variety of social life they enjoyed within the purlieus of the West End, and as they were probably not keen knitters they dreaded the incipient tedium of country life, the majority were refreshingly surprised at the range of activities, social and otherwise, available to them, and very few ever regretted their stay, even though a small minority suffered badly from a viral infection of the hand prevalent in the 50's and 60's which became known locally as 'Brodie Finger' after the name of the male ward where the contamination was thought to be endemic.

Wylie McKissock's first operating theatre with its large, south facing bay window was on the ground floor and was converted from part of the matron's suite and a portion of one of the small adjoining wards. The theatre was small, cramped, and heated by electric wall panels, but it served its purpose well. It was in these surroundings that McKissock demonstrated his characteristic modifications of the principles of neurosurgery to his early trainees, the majority of whom went on to create first class neurosurgical centres either in this country or overseas. Twenty four of his pupils became consultant neurosurgeons and of these fourteen held their appointments in the United Kingdom. Wylie's first trainee was Valentine Logue and he was followed by other well known neurosurgical names such as 'Tickey' Walsh, Alan Richardson, Kenneth Till, Alastair Paterson, John Hankinson, Jason Brice, Ellis Strachan, Ian McCaul, John Garfield, Kenneth Paine, Julian Taylor, Norman Grant, David Uttley, John Daws, 'Rab' Hide, Inderra Bhatti, Sanash Bhagwati, Homi Dastur, Kay de Villiers, Matej Lipovsek, John Blundell and Andrew Talalla.

In addition to the theatre the operating suite contained the scrub up area, sterilising and preparation rooms, as well as a changing room which was used in turn by both the medical and the nursing staff. Patients were anaesthetised and recovered in the theatre itself which was a very inefficient and unsatisfactory business, but the number of patients treated increased rapidly. With just the one theatre, emergency cases always presented a problem and these occasionally had to be dealt with in the adjacent linen room! The case for a purpose built operating suite was overwhelming and eventually one was constructed and opened in 1960 directly below and in front of the old theatre. These new theatres had full modern facilities apart from a recovery room and an intensive care ward, neither of which were deemed to be essential until the late '60s and early '70s. When highly specialised intensive care was shown to bring about an improvement in the outcome of the critically ill neurosurgical patient a small side room was set aside for this purpose until the theatre block was extended to include a fully equipped intensive therapy unit in 1974. In it's day the ITU was the largest neurosurgically dedicated department of it's kind in the UK, and this may well be still the case. This unit was further extended in 1994 when a third theatre was built, at the same time as the original two were up-graded.

One of McKissock's prime objectives as a teacher was to ensure that his trainees adopted standard techniques for each type of case which were economical in terms of time, the use of instruments, and movement, as he strongly adhered to the view that infection was much less likely to occur if an operation was carried out expeditiously. He was also keen to obtain the maximum patient turn over out of his limited number of beds, and to do this he set in place a system which ensured that patients could be returned to their referring hospital as quickly as possible. McKissock made certain that when a patient was discharged from the Atkinson Morley's the referring hospital received a typewritten case sheet complete with clinical history, examination, investigations, operation note and progress reports. After patients were discharged from the outpatient department they continued to receive a follow-up letter from McKissock at intervals asking about their progress, and this type of enquiry would be carried on for the rest of their lives if they had been serious cases. He was very advanced in all aspects of patient care, and did not require politicians or a 'directors of quality' to tell him how to run an efficient unit. He was way ahead of them all! On a visit to him only a week before he died it was terrifying to witness his reactions when we described to him the burgeoning 'directive' industry that is held to be so sacred in the contemporary health service - it was a real flash back to him in his prime. His snort of derision spoke volumes!

Wylie McKissock made sure that his unit did not lag behind in the advance of neurosurgical practice. Amongst a mass of pioneering work in all areas of neurosurgery, he and his colleagues undertook a number of studies on the natural history of sub-arachnoid haemorrhage as a guide to the treatment of intracranial aneurysms. This was probably the first occasion that a controlled scientific study was employed in neurosurgery. The results gave much food for thought to those who were hell-bent on a surgical approach to everything. In 1966 when a large co-operative study was organised by nineteen neurosurgical units in the United States the Atkinson Morley's team was so prominent in this field that they were asked to join as the twentieth; their collaboration was crucial as the department made the largest individual contribution to the study by providing nearly one third of the total number of cases.

During the later part of his working life McKissock's colleagues were Lawrence S. Walsh (1916-1986), and Alan E. Richardson. 'Tickey' Walsh was born and bred in South Africa where he first qualified and worked as a pharmacist as a preliminary to being able to afford to proceed with his medical training. His diminutive stature lead to his nickname 'Tickey' as this was the colloquial name for the smallest coin of the S. African currency; and it was by this affectionate sobriquet that he was universally known, even to his family and many friends. After qualifying with the Gold Medal in medicine for his year he completed his house jobs before setting out on an overland journey through Africa to London, no mean feat in 1947, and he had many exciting adventures on the way. On arrival in UK he became house surgeon to McKissock at the National Hospital, this was his introduction to neurosurgery, and he went on to specialise in this subject under McKissock's aegis, before becoming a Consultant at AMH in 1957. His training included a period of research into the natural history of cerebral aneurysms, and their treatment, both medical and surgical. The pace of work in this field could not be hurried, and many years and other contributors became involved, particularly Alan Richardson when he joined the unit, before these first controlled studies began to yield results which would form the scientific foundations for the modern treatment of sub-arachnoid haemorrhage. Another of Walsh's interests lay in stereotactic surgery, which was used in the treatment of Parkinson's Disease, and he developed a major commitment to the promotion of functional neurosurgery; registrars in training would spend six months with him exclusively occupied in this field, which spilled over into the stereotactic implantation of radioactive material into otherwise inoperable tumours of the pituitary and pineal regions. With the advent of l-dopa and related drugs for the successful treatment of extrapyamidal diseases much of this sort of surgery became temporarily redundant, but its techniques are still valid, and it continues to be employed for the treatment of certain psychiatric states, epilepsy, and tumour biopsy among other neurological conditions.

The third member of the team was Alan Richardson who, in addition to his surgical skills, possessed a mind of great clarity allied to a steely resolve. He complemented McKissock's orderly and organised approach to the way in which the department was run, and the direction in which research interests should be pursued, and he played a vital part in enforcing the rigorous conduct of the aneurysm study protocols. If it sometimes appeared that he was locked in permanent battle with the administration, this was not far from the truth; no one fought harder to preserve the worthwhile products that sprang from the AMH method of running a unit, or to defeat plans for casting aside solid advantages for the sake of currently fashionable administrative theory. No sooner than one problem was overcome, but the next appeared on the horizon: plans to move the unit to some outlandish place had to be scotched; some well-intentioned but inept individual was planning to introduce some new process when there was nothing wrong with the old method, or inhibiting the adoption of new and beneficial techniques. In all these areas Richardson was indefatigable in defending the interests of the hospital; and he was responsible for many improvements in departmental function and hospital development, and all this against a very busy clinical schedule which included a major interest in surgery for spinal degenerative conditions, aneurysms, and functional disorders.

On McKissock's retirement David Uttley was appointed to the staff. His surgical interests included pituitary surgery, skull base surgery and microsurgery in the spine, an honorary appointment at the Royal Marsden Hospital had lead to him meeting members of the Head and Neck unit, as a result he formed a close working relationship with Daniel J. Archer, the maxillo-facial surgeon, over the years which specialised in skull base surgery. Although Uttley has now retired this work has been taken over by Miss Anne Moore, one of the current neurosurgical consultants, the others are Anthony Bell (the founding Professor of the academic department), Henry Marsh, Francis Johnson, and Simon Stapleton, so there are now five consultant posts in the unit. There has been an equivalent increase in the junior staff from the early days; and now there are two senior registrars, four registrars, and three senior house officers. There is also a lecturer who spends much of his time in the laboratories, as a result of this growing academic influence closer ties have been forged with the Medical School, to mutual advantage. Over the past decade links have been established with the University of Washington, in Seattle. This is claimed to be the largest Medical School in North America, and the Neurosurgical Division under it's head, Professor H. Richard Winn is of a corresponding size, with staffing to the same scale. Residents from the department come over to work at AMH for a year at a time, currently two are present at one time but overlap by six months; and all the visitors have gone back with enhanced experience, most of them having made friends for life with their UK counterparts. This transatlantic bridge is not just one way: the members of the British team, if they are wise, learn a good deal from their American cousins, and the Seattle Department is always helpful when someone from AMH wants to do research, or study some particular surgical technique which is not readily available elsewhere. The year at AMH is eagerly awaited by the American residents, and has been from its inception an official part of their training programme.

Life at AMH under McKissock's regime was not all work, there was a light-hearted side to things, as there must be in any well run organisation, and he was very much aware that the staff needed some relaxation and encouragement. Juniors were warned that they may be swept up at a moments notice at midday on Saturday and taken out to lunch at the 'Dog and Fox' in Wimbledon village, or the 'Fairmile' near Cobham, where he always proved to be a very generous host. Ill-health in later years brought a halt to these spontaneous extravagances, but he founded a Photographic Club at the Hospital which was open to all the medical staff: meetings were monthly and took the form of a competition. The year culminated in a splendid annual dinner in the Hospital where one's unalloyed pleasure was attended by a frisson of anxiety lest he insist, quite erroneously, that one had been begging him for an opportunity to address one's fellow diners – it was the only time that his otherwise flawless memory failed him! The best tradition was the Christmas morning punch, which he made and served in the operating theatre corridor at 11 a.m.; four gallons, made to a secret recipe, were brewed, and consumed within the hour. The start of the festivities was timed to coincide with the completion of Father Christmas's round with his attendant fairies, and this was always recognised as being thirsty work. This event was open to all the staff, and many made a special effort to come into the hospital and bring their families for this cheerful interlude, which was followed by the patients' lunch on the wards and the ceremonial carving of turkeys. It was the only occasion in the year when the whole staff could congregate together, and probably some contacts were only reinforced at this annual party; it would start very quietly, and there would be some concern that no one was going to turn up, and then there would be a gradual crescendo of voices and laughter until noon. It was and remains an excellent way to start the day. McKissock began the tradition in the 1940s, and when he retired Walsh took over the responsibility for a few years, before handing over to Uttley who in turn recently installed Miss Moore in the role of punch-maker for what should prove to be a long period of tenure.

When neurosurgery first began at the Atkinson Morley's the anaesthetics were administered by David Aserman who had worked with McKissock at both Maida Vale and Leavesden, and Dr. Barman, who left to go into general practice in 1944. In 1945 Donald Blatchley and then, one year later, Sheila Anderson were invited to join the anaesthetic staff. Sheila Anderson who had graduated at the Royal Free Hospital in 1937 was a consultant at Great Ormond Street where she had worked with McKissock, and it was he who persuaded to her to come and work with him at the Atkinson Morley's. Unlike Blatchley and Aserman who had rather drifted into anaesthetics, Anderson had set her sights on a career in anaesthesia from the time she qualified, and with her evolving skills she was able to introduce newer techniques into the anaesthetic practice at the hospital. She was a good teacher and a loyal supporter of all of those who pulled their weight, but was quite capable of visiting choice verbal reprimands on those she felt were lazy. The paediatric laryngoscope she designed with Sir Ivan Magill is still in everyday use. Other anaesthetic consultants over the years have included W.W. Deane, Norman Trapps, David Coleman, Eddie Berwick, Terry Gould, Alex Thurlow, Tom Hollway, Maryke Krayenbrink, Professor George Hall, Plat Razis, Joan Desborough and Beverly Sutton. In the early days neurosurgical procedures were carried out under inhalational anaesthetic techniques with the patients spontaneously breathing nitrous oxide, oxygen, and either trilene or ether, but in the 1960's anaesthetic practice was changed, patients were paralysed with relaxant drugs such as tubocurarine and mechanically ventilated with anaesthetic gases supplemented with a narcotic. This change allied to the pharmacological control of blood pressure were such major advances in anaesthetic practice that operating conditions were transformed, and thus permitted the introduction of complicated neurosurgical procedures (such as the clipping of aneurysms for example) which could now be undertaken with increased safety. Later, the development of the operating microscope, which combined variable magnification with brilliant illumination, lead surgeons to become ever more precise in facilitating the resolution of complicated lesions with a corresponding fall in the risk of damage to neighbouring vital structures.

St. George's appointed Theodore Crawford in 1946 to the chair of Pathology, its first professor and academic department. Crawford had a special interest in neuropathology and encouraged the development of good neuropathological support at the Atkinson Morley's. Crawford and McKissock were bound by a mutual regard for the other's abilities, and no one was better pleased than the latter when Crawford received a knighthood for his services to pathology after being President of the Royal College of Pathologists and Vice-President of the Cancer Research Campaign. It was not always easy to find pathologists with a special interest in neuropathology but Rufus Crompton who ran the department initially, and more recently Peter Wilkins, who has brought the whole department, lock, stock and barrel back to Wimbledon as well as considerably extending it, have been worthy successors.

The long serving Miss Gale, who used to wander around the wards and grounds in the company of her dog, retired as Matron in 1948 and was replaced by Miss Guest, who in turn was replaced in 1956 by Miss Mary Lee Abbott who continued in post until 1972. In 1968 the Salmon Report did away with the concept of Matron and with it abolished the distinctive uniform; the new title became the 'Senior Nursing Officer', then this form of address was dropped, and the most senior nurse in the hospital now became known as the 'Director of Nursing.' Cynics would say that the changes in title have been reflected in uncertainties surrounding the true nature of the role, and it is perhaps a sign that the tinkering process has gone full circle when one hears the name Matron making a reappearance in the 1990s (together with the awe-inspiring uniform!). Misses Thursby Coombes, West and Anderson have filled this post at AMH in recent years under the various styles and titles as they were successively introduced.

In 1949 ward names were introduced at the Atkinson Morley's. The male neurosurgical ward on the ground floor was named *Brodie* and the female neurosurgical ward at the opposite end of the hospital was named *Hawkins*, a name that was replaced by *McKissock* in the late '80s. The latter was delighted, and derived great satisfaction from it as he was the only person, as far as he was aware, who had been so honoured in his lifetime.

Brodie was named after Sir Benjamin Brodie (1793-1862), the St. George's surgeon who was largely responsible for the founding of the medical school and who also introduced the examination for the Fellowship of the Royal College of Surgeons. He became President of the Royal College of Surgeons, the Royal Society and the General Medical Council. Hawkins ward took its name from Charles Hawkins whose details have been outlined previously.

The basement or convalescent wards were named *Kent* after the Duke and Duchess of Kent who were patrons to the hospital, and *Baillie* after Matthew Baillie (1761-1823), a physician to St. George's from 1787-1800. Baillie, who had the good fortune to be the nephew of John Hunter, was the apple of William Hunter's eye and heir to his estate. He was a pupil at St. George's and elected to the medical staff in 1787. After his marriage to Sophia, the daughter of Dr. Denman, the obstetrician, he was referred many patients by his father-in-law and then in 1798 he took over the practice of Pitcairn, the St. Bartholomew's Physician. His large and lucrative practice which brought him in over ten thousand pounds a year, interfered with his duties at St. George's and lead to his resignation after only twelve years in post. The east top floor ward which was used for female psychiatry was given the name of *Bernhard Baron* after one of the great philanthropists of the twentieth century. His was the archetypal rags-to-riches life story. Born in Russia of French origin Baron emigrated to America at the age of 17 where he worked as a tobacco cutter. He eventually began his own cigarette making business which he developed into the giant Carreras company. Baron moved part of his company to England where he made such brands as Craven A, Black Cat, Piccadilly and Turf. His fabulous wealth enabled him to indulge his passion for donating money to hospitals, orphanages, and homes for the disabled. During his lifetime he gave away over £3,000,000, which included donations to St. George's in 1928, the Bolingbroke Hospital, and the Victoria Children's Hospital. *Timothy Holmes* was the name chosen for the male psychiatric ward, but Desmond Curran, for reasons best known to himself, objected strongly. Timothy Holmes, a former St. George's surgeon who had served the hospital well had been in his day a Vice-President of the Royal College of Surgeons, first Dean of the Medical School and then Treasurer as well as a highly respected surgeon. Holmes was said to be 'open in his opinions, highly respected and a formidable examiner' to the degree that his name was borrowed for the repeatable mnemonic (there is another version!) which is familiar with all students 'Timothy doth vex all very nervous pupils'. Such are the vagaries of the medical staff at St. George's that Holmes' name is barely remembered, yet Baillie's name still warrants a ward name at the Hospital!. The Governors reluctantly deferred to Curran allowing him his rather curious choice of *Young,* after Thomas 'Phenomenon' Young, the St. George's physician, who was said to be one of the greatest intellects of his day, but who was considered to be a bad teacher of medicine and alleged to be not even interested in the subject! The children's ward was named *Rosebery* after Lord Rosebery, the Scottish statesman, who was Chairman of the London County Council and a Derby winner thrice as well as being a Governor of St. George's, and who became Liberal Prime Minister in 1894 after Gladstone's death,. Later, when the new basement theatres were opened, *Baillie* ward was converted into neurosurgical office accommodation, but it's name was used to replace *Bernhard Baron* on the top floor, and his name was bestowed on the children's ward, in place of Rosebery, who dropped out of the list. After Desmond Curran's retirement his own name replaced that of Baillie.

Wylie McKissock encouraged all departments to take on an active teaching role. As his reputation grew the number of his own trainees increased rapidly, and there was an urgent need to find them accommodation. An attempt was made in 1949 to purchase 'The Firs' – a large house which stood directly to the west of the hospital in Copse Hill, but the Governors were outbid by a Mr. Ellison, who eventually withdrew his bid, and after the hospital gave him £100 to compensate him for his legal expenses, they were able to purchase 'The Firs' for £5,000 the following year.

'The Firs' had been built in 1853 and was of great historical interest for two reasons. Firstly, it was in fact two dwellings which shared a common living room and had been built as an experiment in communal living. The original owners were John Ludlow and Thomas Hughes who were both members of the Christian Scientist Movement and were of the view that communal living would be of social and educational benefit to their young families. Its second claim to fame was that Thomas Hughes wrote 'Tom Brown's Schooldays' whilst he was resident there as an example to his own son, who was just about to go away to public school. Later it was owned by Madame de Graz, a French aristocrat. After it was purchased 'The Firs' provided accommodation for both junior medical staff and students for nearly two decades. It also served as a sports pavilion in the late 50's after the second sports pavilion burnt down, and as an outpatient clinic for Dr. John Penman a neurologist who had been invited by McKissock to develop methods for the treatment of trigeminal neuralgia. The final metamorphosis of this part of Copse Hill took place in the mid-60s when The Firs was demolished and replaced by purpose built flats bearing the same name, which expanded the on-site living accommodation available for junior doctors, senior nurses, and other staff. These opened for occupation during the last week of December 1966, and were regarded at that time as setting the national standard for this type of residential provision. Those who had been hospital residents prior to this certainly appreciated what seemed to them to be the ultimate in spacious luxury. The number of units of accommodation was further increased in 1948 when the Governors took a lease on Birch Lodge which was attached to Possil House, and it was ultimately purchased outright in 1954.

James Bull (1911-1987), who was invited by Wylie McKissock to develop a department of neuroradiology at AMH, was born in Buckinghamshire and educated at Repton, Gonville and Caius College, Cambridge, and St. George's Hospital Medical School. After qualifying he began to specialise in radiology, and during his training he met McKissock who persuaded him to go to the Seraphimer Hospital in Stockholm to study neuroradiology under Erik Lysholm. The two radiologists became great friends. In 1939 Bull returned to London and was appointed radiologist to the Maida Vale Hospital. He joined the RAMC in 1940, first working at the Head Injury Hospital in Oxford before he was posted to the Far East, where he was captured and taken as a Prisoner of War on the fall of Singapore. He spent three and a half dreadful years of starvation and torture in the notorious Changi Prison. After surviving this period of extreme deprivation he could never accept any contact with the Japanese; and although he never spoke of his suffering, he donated his war diary to the Imperial War Museum. As soon as he was repatriated he returned to Sweden to work with Erik Lindgren at the Karolinska Hospital on percutaneous angiography and pneumoencephalography. In 1946 James Bull joined McKissock at the Atkinson Morley's Hospital and then in 1947 at the National Hospital for Nervous Diseases. He lead the field in the development of neuroradiology in Great Britain. Over six feet in height, handsome, with an imposing presence and stentorian voice Bull built up a large internationally recognised neuroradiology department at the Atkinson Morley's.

As the speciality developed the equipment essential for the radiological investigation of neurological disease became ever more complicated and elaborate, so more and more space was given over to the department, which was situated in the basement. It became one of the busiest neuroradiological departments in the world and by 1958 it was carrying out more than 1,000 percutaneous angiographic studies a year. In addition to his other gifts Bull was a fine teacher and attracted many first rate junior radiologists who wished to learn from him. One of the first of these was James Ambrose, a South African, a spitfire fighter pilot during the war, who in 1975 took over the department after James Bull suffered a coronary thrombosis. If the latter could be said to have laid the foundations of international repute for the department Ambrose made certain that it achieved world wide acclaim. He and Geoffrey Hounsfield, now Sir Geoffrey and a Nobel Prize Winner for Medicine in 1979, developed Computerised Tomography at the Atkinson Morley's Hospital. In 1971 the very first patient was successfully scanned and within a short time the neuroradiological world beat a path to the hospital's door; to see this wonderful non-invasive technique; that original machine now rests on its laurels in the National Science Museum. The next marvel was Magnetic Resonance Imaging, which depends for its effect on scanning patients in changing magnetic fields as its name implies, and where, for the first time, potentially damaging radiation is not required. Despite the fact that AMH was one of the UK's busiest units , with an exceptional record of innovation, the Department of Health would not purchase an MRI machine for the hospital but this lamentable deficiency was circumvented by the entrepreneurial brother of James Byrne, one of the consultant radiologists at the time, agreeing to finance an MRI Unit within the grounds of the hospital. This unit now provides both a general and a neurological imaging service for a large part of the South Thames Region. James Ambrose retired in 1988, and this large department with its two CT scanners is now staffed by Geoff Hart, Juliet Britton and Andy Clifton.

The department of psychiatry was established at the Atkinson Morley's in 1946 by Desmond Curran (1903-1985). Curran was born in Devon and educated at Wellington, Trinity College, Cambridge, and St. George's Hospital Medical School. After qualifying in 1928, Curran, who could well have become an eminent physician, chose to follow a career in psychiatry and was appointed a house physician at the Bethlem in 1928, and then at Maida Vale. From there he travelled to Baltimore where he worked under Adolf Meyer. Curran developed his own practical style in the diagnosis and treatment of psychiatric illness. Anthony Feiling showed great foresight when he paved the way for Curran's appointment to the consultant staff of St. George's in 1934 at the tender age of thirty one. On the outbreak of war in 1939 Curran was called up into the Royal Navy, and became the youngest Surgeon Captain in the service, and by 1945 was recognised as being at the forefront of a rapidly expanding and increasingly important speciality. On Curran's return to St. George's, he was invited by McKissock to join him at Wimbledon. There was some opposition from certain sources at Hyde Park Corner but Curran nevertheless came to the AMH where in June 1945 he opened a large female ward, and six male beds which were accommodated in side rooms. On her youthful appointment as matron to St. George's at the age of 33 in 1947, Muriel Powell immediately forbade young student nurses from going on to the male psychiatric ward! This was an astonishing decision in view of Curran's eminence and Miss Powell's well-known humanitarian outlook. It took some determined persuasion from Curran before finally she relented and gave her permission for student nurses to look after psychiatrically disturbed male patients. From then on until her retirement in 1969, when she was appointed Chief Nurse in Scotland, and created Dame, Muriel Powell did all that she could to support the development of psychiatry at the Atkinson Morley's. In 1947 the other large convalescent ward on the top floor of the hospital ceased to function as such and was converted into the male psychiatric ward. The department so formed became only the second inpatient psychiatric unit to be opened within a teaching hospital – the first being at Guy's Hospital.

Curran, tall, kind, witty, humorous, highly intelligent, urbane and erudite, soon managed to attract Maurice Partridge (1910-1984) and Sir Paul Mallinson (1909-1980) to join him at St. George's and AMH to create the foundations for the development of a psychiatric department which was to become pre-eminent among medical schools and gain a well deserved international reputation. Desmond Curran, as well as serving St. George's for over thirty years was a member of the Franklin Committee on punishment in prisons and borstals, and the Wolfenden Commission on homosexuality. He served also as adviser in psychiatry to the Foreign and Home Offices and as president of both the psychiatric section of the Royal Society of Medicine and the Royal Medico-Psychological Association. In 1961 Curran was appointed the first professor of psychiatry at St. George's Hospital, and was awarded a CBE. Under his aegis the new department flourished, and his teaching to both under- and post-graduates, together with that of Partridge and Mallinson was clear, practical, and meticulous in clinical detail. He inspired others and it is a fitting tribute to him that the department he created at St. George's and the Atkinson Morley's continues to expand and thrive, and is noted for its clinical and academic excellence. Curran, of course, could not have created such a department without the support and loyalty of his two colleagues.

The junior member of the team, Maurice Partridge, was educated at

Shrewsbury, Balliol College, Oxford, and Guy's Hospital for which he always retained great affection, and indeed he continued to live in rooms in the Warden's House there until he retired from St. George's in 1970. After qualifying Partridge worked at the Johns Hopkins in Baltimore before serving in the war as a Lieutenant Commander in the Royal Navy. After demobilisation he worked at St. Andrew's Hospital in Northampton before joining Curran at AMH in 1951. Partridge was a superb teacher and justly popular with the students who were attracted to his rather eccentric and untidy appearance. With a nervous tic of his facial muscles, he was always peering out behind a dense haze of cigarette smoke; he wore thick and hairy country tweed suits whatever the season with a large coloured handkerchief dangling from the breast pocket. He was a co-author with Curran of a very popular textbook called 'Psychological Medicine' which Curran had first written with Erich Guttmann, and which was edited in more recent times by Peter Storey who trained under Curran and Partridge. Maurice Partridge was keenly interested in pre-frontal leucotomy as a treatment for certain types of psychiatric illness, and he worked very closely with McKissock in this field. After their retirement the interest in psychosurgery at AMH was maintained by Alan Richardson and Desmond Kelly, who moved away from the crude pre-frontal leucotomy to develop stereotatic limbic lesions which were more precise and accurate.

Maurice Partridge, or as he was popularly known 'The Bird', was a most amusing man and a great story teller. Desperately shy, he shunned invitations to speak at large dinners but he was much in demand as a popular after dinner speaker in more familiar and intimate gatherings. For someone who like his senior, Curran, chain-smoked cigarettes, Partridge was a very athletic man who regularly played squash against the students. On such occasions he usually resorted to gamesmanship, so that even on the hottest of days he would appear on the court wearing a sweater, and was quite likely to leave the court between sets to don another one!. Such an action invariably demoralised far fitter and superior opposition.

After retirement Partridge lived in Suffolk, but travelled widely to exotic and remote places around the world. He kept in touch with his colleagues at St. George's by postcard. His handwriting was microscopic and he seemed to be able to cram countless paragraphs on to the back of the card signing himself, as he always did, with a small wavy line which resembled the silhouette of a distant bird in flight, presumably a partridge.

It seemed only natural for William Paul Mallinson to join Curran at AMH in 1946 as they had served together in the Navy during the war, and each nursed an admiration for the other's abilities. Mallinson, educated at Westminster School, Christ Church, Oxford, and St. Thomas's Hospital Medical School gained a Rockefeller scholarship in 1939 before serving as a Lieutenant Commander in the Royal Naval Volunteer Reserve from 1940-1946. Immediately he was demobilised Sir Paul Mallinson, as he had become after succeeding as the third holder of the baronetcy in 1944, was appointed a Consultant Psychiatrist to St. George's Hospital to join Curran. Both as a duo and later a trio, with the arrival of Maurice Partridge, they formed a happy, harmonious and united partnership. As soon as he arrived at the Atkinson Morley's Mallinson opened his Insulin Coma Unit, and when the psychiatric out-patients department was opened at No.15 Knightsbridge he intro-duced electro-convulsive therapy. This was the first time that this form of treatment for depressive illness had been used in a teaching hospital. The anaesthetics for the ECT sessions were usually administered by the junior anaesthetist assisted by a nurse and a porter! The patients were walked in turn to a small room, where they lay on a trolley bed and were given a small dose of an intravenous anaesthetic agent and a muscle relaxant. The psychiatrist would next enter the room, apply the electrodes to the head, administer the electric shock and then leave. At this point it was the responsibility of the unfortunate anaesthetist and the porter (perhaps better fitted to the role), using any means available, to transfer the patient to an adjoining large room and on to a mattress lying on the floor where the victim could 'sleep off' the effects of the treatment. Sometimes there would be more than twenty patients asleep on the floor at the end of a session! Just occasionally it might have crossed the anaesthetist's mind to wonder what the previous owner of the house, Robert Stephenson Baden-Powell, the founder of the Boy Scout Movement, would have made of it if he had seen his former bedroom and dressing room looking for all the world like the morning after some particularly wild debauch.

The pipe smoking, tall, and modest Sir Paul appeared on first acquaintance to be serious, dour, ponderous and the least approachable member of the trio but it was soon evident that he was a quiet, self-critical man who had an unhurried and painstakingly careful approach to the clinical diagnosis and treatment of psychiatric illness. He had a wicked, dry sense of humour, and was extremely popular with both under- and postgraduates who appreciated his teaching, admired his clinical skills, and valued his advice and friendship.

Outside St. George's Sir Paul examined in psychiatry for the Royal College of Physicians, was civilian consultant to the Royal Navy, and became vice president of the psychiatric section of the Royal Society of Medicine, as well as having a busy private practice in Wimpole Street. Away from medicine altogether Sir Paul took an active interest in the family's international timber business and eventually became chairman. The business was based in the Isle of Wight where he had a house in which he loved entertaining his junior colleagues and their families, and it was close to Cowes where he enjoyed the sailing.

The reputations of Curran, Mallinson and Partridge as leaders in the field of psychiatry and their excellence as teachers of the subject attracted a large number of able registrars such as Peter Hays, Peter Storey, Brian O'Connell, Michael Raymond, Robert Priest, and Arthur Crisp who all went on to become eminent psychiatrists in their own right.

Despite Curran's initial doubts as to the value of psychotherapy and psychology he accepted that his personal prejudices should not stand in their way so he established departments in both subjects, psychotherapists and psychologists became an integral part of the team involved in the treatment of psychiatric illness. It was not long before the psychologists began to work closely with the neurosurgeons and their importance was generally accepted. If Curran was alive today he would be quick to set aside his earlier misgivings and would be delighted that there is now a chair in psychology at St. George's.

When Curran retired in 1967 he was as succeeded as Professor by Arthur Crisp, who built on the foundations laid by his predecessors in expanding the department of psychiatry at the Atkinson Morley's into one of the largest psychiatric treatment centres in Europe, so much so that it now boasts five professors in various branches of psychiatry.

Under Arthur Crisp's guidance the department is now recognised as a centre of excellence for the treatment of eating disorders, drug and solvent abuse, learning disabilities and sleep disorders. Arthur Crisp has been ably supported by his colleagues who have included Desmond Kelly, Char-Nie Chen, Aggrey Burke, John Cobb, Professor Tom Burns, R.S. Kalucy, John Kellett, Desmond Kelly, Professor Hubert Lacey, Paul O'Farrell, Stuart Lieberman, James Watson, Malcolm Pines, Andrew Powell, and Michael Humphrey.

When Wylie McKissock was at Leavesden he recognised the importance of having first class specialists in ophthalmology and neurology as part of his team, and in fact he continued to encourage allied disciplines to work with him throughout his career. At Leavesden he enjoyed working with Sir Francis Walshe, the neurologist and Sir Allen Goldsmith, the ophthalmogist. After the move of McKissock's unit to the Atkinson Morley's, Alexander Galbraith Cross, who was the ophthalmologist to St. Mary's Hospital and by a stroke of good fortune a near neighbour in Copse Hill, agreed to take over from Goldsmith, and would visit willingly on Sunday mornings. He continued to provide a service to the neurosurgical unit until 1967 when Patrick Holme-Sellors was appointed consultant ophthalmologist to St. George's. In recent years Graham Thompson has been the visiting ophthalmologist. Neuro-otology was also very close to McKissock's heart and a small cubby-hole in the basement was converted for use as a sound-proof examination room; it contained audiological facilities as well as the equipment for caloric studies of vestibular function, as these were of great importance in the diagnosis of posterior fossa lesions in the days prior to CT and MRI scans. The occupants of this rather eerie chamber were the ENT surgeons from St. George's Hospital. The first incumbent was Brian Pickard, whose laconic style was entirely in keeping with his sporadic visitations, and he was followed by David Whittam who still consults at the hospital by request.

After the war Sir Francis Walshe who had by then returned to his post at University College Hospital agreed to visit AMH once a week and provide neurological support to McKissock's unit. He was supported by Anthony Feiling, Alan Barham-Carter and St.J. Elkington. Elkington and Feiling were both on the staff of Maida Vale, Elkington was also on

98

the staff of St. Thomas's, and Feiling, who had previously worked at AMH as visiting physician, was consultant neurologist to St. George's and a past dean of the Medical School; but by this time it was clear that a more substantial and supportive neurological presence was required in Wimbledon. The opportunity to expand the frontiers of the neuroscience department in this direction came about with the appointment of Denis John Williams as consultant neurologist to St. George's Hospital in 1946. Williams was born in Aberaeron in Wales and educated at Manchester Grammar School, and Manchester University where he qualified in 1932, before entering Harvard as a Rockefeller fellow. In 1936 he joined the Royal Air Force and served throughout the Second World War as a Wing Commander. When he left the services in 1945 he was appointed civilian consultant to the RAF and continued in this post until 1972. As well as being appointed to St. George's in 1946 he had similar appointments at the National Hospital for Nervous Diseases, and King Edward VII Hospital for Officers. It was agreed on his appointment to St. George's that his inpatient beds would be at AMH. Wylie McKissock was keen that some of the convalescent beds in the basement should be given over to neurology but the consultants at St. George's were loathe to surrender these beds so neurology had to be accommodated within the precious neurosurgical bed complement – a sure indication as to the degree of importance McKissock attached to the ideal of having all aspects of the neurosciences under one roof. As a result McKissock was forced to relinquish eight male and eight female beds – a rare defeat for him; but this was only a battle not the war, and he very quickly wore down the opposition at Hyde Park Corner, so that soon neurology was able to occupy it's own wards in the basement.

Denis Williams was intensely proud of his Welsh roots and went to great pains to retain the soft, lilting speech of his homeland through-out his life. Flamboyant, egotistical, silver haired, distinguished in appearance, and often sporting a buttonhole carnation Williams was highly theatrical in his manner and presentation. He bore a faint resemblance not only in appearance but in performance to Emlyn Williams (1905-1987) the well known Welsh actor, playwright and producer. In many ways Denis Williams was a latter day James Collier and had a battery of gestures such as fluttering his eyelids and rolling his eyes whilst making a point, but was nevertheless a superb teacher and an outstanding clinician. He was highly respected within his speciality and was a Vice-President of the Royal College of Physicians, president of the Neurology section of the Royal Society of Medicine, president of the Association of British Neurologists, and founder and vice president of the British Epilepsy Association. Denis Williams loved ceremony and tradition, and as well as being a member of the Saville and Wayfarers Clubs, he was a Freeman of the City of London, and a Liveryman of the Worshipful Society of Apothecaries, but he loved to get away from things and go back to his dairy and sheep farm in his beloved Wales. At AMH he helped lay firm foundations for the future of neurology, and was one of the first to establish an electroencephalography unit, using an early four channel recorder which he had brought back from the United States for use in his own consulting rooms. For many years the presiding genius of this department was Miss Monica Davitt B.A. the senior technician, who not only prepared the records but often was willing to give a preliminary report on them as well. Denis Williams was awarded the CBE in 1954 and resigned from Atkinson Morley's in 1970.

Some five years after his own appointment Denis Williams gained a junior colleague in the shape of John Hamilton Paterson and the two proved to be an effective team for the best part of ten years. Although they were both excellent doctors and attentive to the needs of their patients, in other respects they were as different as chalk and cheese. Paterson was of a quiet and modest disposition, and totally committed to the Atkinson Morley's and his responsibilities as a teacher.

John Hamilton Paterson (1915-1962) was born in Kuling, Kiangshi, China, the son of two medical missionaries. He was educated at University College and University College Hospital where he qualified in 1939. Before joining the Royal Army Medical Corps he worked for eighteen months at Leavesden with Wylie McKissock. Paterson was then posted to the Military Hospital for Head Injuries in St. Hugh's College, Oxford where he first met and worked with Denis Williams. After a brief period at Oxford Paterson was posted as a neurologist to the army and served in France, Belgium and Delhi. On demobilisation in 1946 he returned to University College Hospital as a registrar to Sir Francis Walshe who was still visiting the Atkinson Morley's every week. In 1948 Paterson was appointed as neurological registrar to the National Hospital for Nervous Diseases, Queen's Square, and on completion of this post accepted one as a psychiatric registrar to round out his training. He was appointed Assistant Neurological Physician to St. George's Hospital in 1951 and immediately took on the major burden for the teaching of neurology at the AMH. His opinion was frequently sought and highly regarded by his colleagues. Under- and post-graduates found his teaching to be interesting, relaxed, yet precise, and encompassed an enormous range. Appropriately he was sub-dean of the Institute of Neurology from 1957 to 1962 and it was a great tragedy when he was struck down by illness which led to his untimely death at the early age of 47. John Hamilton Paterson's death was a devastating loss to the hospital and the medical school.

Peter Gautier Smith was appointed Consultant Neurologist in 1963 to replace Paterson but after twelve years he resigned his appointment to devote all of his energies to the National Hospital, where he had become Dean. When Denis Williams resigned in 1970, Pauline Munro, the senior registrar in the department, was promoted to the vacant consultant post, and for the first time this was made a full time appointment. within the St. George's group, so the potential for divided allegiances was eradicated. Under her leadership the department of neurology implemented the Neurological Advisory Committee's recommendations that all consultant neurological appointments should have direct access to full neurological investigatory facilities. Closer links were forged with the surrounding district general hospitals. Neurology was recognised as a sub-regional speciality and all consultant appointments to the district general hospitals were made joint appointments with the Atkinson Morley's. David Kendall who had been consultant neurologist to St. Helier Hospital was given an honorary appointment to St. George's, and John Meadows was given a part-time appointment between the Atkinson Morley's, Epsom and St. Helier. Maurice Gross was appointed to the Atkinson Morley's, Kingston and Ashford post. In 1979 there was a further juggling of sessions to ensure that the appointments were only split between the AMH and one district general hospital. This was a far cry from the days when the hospital had been looked after by two part-time consultants; naturally this policy lead to considerable expansion in the consultant ranks, and subsequent Consultant appointments have included Ronald McKeran, Stephen Wilson, Frederick Schon, David Barnes, Yvonne Hart, Carlos de Sousa, Oliver Foster and Damian Wren. By 1977 the need for a full-time neuro-physiologist was recognised, which lead to the appointment of Martin Schwartz (a reversal of the Trans-Atlantic brain drain!) whose remit embraced both the electo-myography and the electro-encephalography departments. Due to an ever increasing work load he has been recently joined by Hamid Modares who is another consultant neurophysiologist. In the early '80s a senior lecturer post in neurology was approved by the University of London, and Nigel Leigh who is now a Professor of Neurology at King's College Hospital was the first holder. Martin Brown is the present Senior Lecturer.

There are now 12 neurologists attached to AMH and surrounding hospitals, with a corresponding major improvement in the width and depth of the service they provide. For nearly thirty years neurology was contained within the gloomy sixteen bedded basement ward which had originally been built as the Women's Day Room. The need for a new and larger ward was clearly apparent to everyone involved, but those who had the power to change things were not listening. By this time the consensus approach to management had produced a bureaucracy grown so swollen and bloated that it had difficulty keeping in contact with its component parts let alone dealing with other matters. The Board of Governors had gone by the wayside and been replaced by an Area Health Authority, which was responsible to a Regional Health Authority, which in turn reported to the Department of Health. St. George's and the Atkinson Morley's were 'managed' by a District Management Team which was accountable to the Area Health Authority. The latter, which though full of its own importance was in reality totally bereft of either vision or drive, felt it's duty was to interfere continually in a nit-picking, inhibitory way in local matters, so the seemingly interminable discussions and arguments concerning the building of a new neurology ward were acrimonious and Byzantine in their complexity. This is not to say that neurology was particularly singled out for this negative discrimination, for to be absolutely fair everything which came within the ambit of the AHA suffered the same fate. The majority of the clinicians at the Atkinson Morley's felt that the opportunity should be seized to completely redesign the hospital by building neurosurgical wards on top of the neurological ward on the land at the back of the present hospital, while preserving the facade and using the space created in the existing part for clinics, offices, and a day case investigation unit, but it proved impossible to convince the Authority of the wisdom and desirability of such a scheme. After many delays in what passed for a planning process the new thirty bedded Kent ward was built in 1979, and situated adjacent to the old one which was converted into offices and consulting rooms. The cost? Much the same as it would have taken to have built the original development as proposed only a very few years earlier!

Wylie McKissock was from his very early days as a neurosurgeon aware of the importance of good occupational therapy and physiotherapy in the rehabilitation of patients who had suffered the disabling effects of a brain injury or other neurological disease. When he arrived at the Atkinson Morley's in 1942 he was surprised to find a small occupational therapy department already in existence. This department had been established in 1939 by the Ladies Committee but by 1942 the ladies were hard pressed to find the necessary resources for its continued support. McKissock ensured that proper funding was made available by the Emergency Medical Service to develop complete departments of physiotherapy and occupational therapy. Ideally both departments required purpose built accommodation but as usual space was at a premium. The local suffragan bishop was approached for his permission to use the chapel for occupational therapy on weekdays, but the healing hand of the church would not countenance such a proposal, so occupational therapy was placed in a Nissen hut which was situated close to the present canteen. Nissen huts were forerunners of the present day Portakabins and had been introduced in the second world war as living and sleeping accommodation for the troops. The Nissen hut was replaced in 1960 with a much larger structure, which was still unmistakably a 'hut', containing a small 'flat' consisting of a bedroom, kitchen, bath, toilet etc. for assessment and training in the activities of daily living.

Physiotherapy was accommodated in the original female dining room on the basement floor of the hospital. The workload of this department has expanded enormously over the years to encompass not only work in the gym, but more acute types of involvement in the wards, and particularly in the ITU where their skills are of crucial importance. Both departments provided excellent acute services to the neurosurgical, neurological and psychiatric patients but Wylie McKissock was intent on establishing a purpose built centre where neurologically disabled patients could be assessed, and then undergo a comprehensive rehabilitation programme under the supervision of a multi-disciplinary team. McKissock was well aware that such a scheme would receive only lukewarm support from the Department of Health, which appeared to be in the grip of terminal stasis, and controlled at that time by the politics of envy. Certainly it was not keen on funding any hospital developments, especially those that were associated with teaching hospitals, however laudable the purpose. So he made an application to the Wolfson Foundation who awarded him £250,000, the largest research grant that the Foundation had ever made, and by some strange quirk the money was given to him personally. It was many years before the implications sank in, but in the general euphoria of the occasion the Board of Governors were naturally delighted and readily made available the piece of land for the building which stands between the Atkinson Morley's and 'The Firs', and which at that time had been leased for many years to an ex-army officer as the premises for his riding school. The Wolfson Rehabilitation Centre was opened in 1967 by Princess Marina, the Duchess of Kent. The building contained forty eight units of residential accommodation, three gymnasia, a hydrotherapy pool, two workshops (heavy and light), a fully equipped domestic unit, a speech therapy unit as well as other essential facilities.

Alan Richardson readily agreed to take on the part-time medical directorship of the centre in addition to his duties as neurosurgeon to the parent hospital. When Alan Richardson relinquished the directorship in the early 70's there were a number of short term or locum appointments until David Jenkins was appointed as medical director of the centre in 1976. The creation of a specialised Rehabilitation Centre attached to a hospital was unique at that time and there is a poignant irony in the fact that plans for the future re-siting of Atkinson Morley's turn the clock back more than a quarter of a century in separating the hospital from it's rehabilitation facility. The Wolfson Centre was the culmination of Wylie McKissock's vision of transforming the Atkinson

Morley's Hospital into a world famous neuroscience centre. The marvel of it all is that it was accomplished during an extremely exacting clinical career, in the space of which he had helped to establish first class departments in neurology, psychiatry, radiology, anaesthesia, neuropathology, rehabilitation, occupational therapy, physiotherapy and medical physics as well as laboratory and pharmacy services. He took an active interest in the school of nursing, the library, the domestic, portering and catering services, the switchboard, the Amandus Club and the estate. As well as his work at the Atkinson Morley's McKissock was actively involved in the affairs of St. George's Hospital and for many years served on the Board of Governors and was chairman of both the Medical Advisory Committee and the Joint Planning Committee for the building of the new St. George's Hospital at Tooting. He was never one of the 'smoke – filled room' variety of committee man, and his intolerance of beating about the bush and making policy 'off the top of one's head' was well known; to get things done a clear, closely argued objective was presented, and woe betide those who came to the meeting unprepared as they were swept aside in a rather cavalier fashion, accompanied by a withering glare over the top of his half moon spectacles. In addition to what may be considered to have been a full-time commitment to AMH, McKissock also held consultant appointments at the National Hospital, Queen's Square, the Hospital for Sick Children, Great Ormond Street, and, in his early days, to many hospitals in southern England and as far afield as Wales. Many of these were psychiatric centres where during the course of his peripatetic wanderings he carried out innumerable leucotomies whilst they were in vogue. He and his team would literally roll up the carpet and get on with things! In recognition of his services he was awarded the OBE in 1946, and deservedly knighted in 1971, just prior to his retirement to his home overlooking Loch Gairloch in Wester Ross, a region he had been going to ever since his honeymoon, where he was able to enjoy his garden, ornithology, wine, cigars and good food. The only thing he probably missed in retirement was the opportunity to tease and outwit bureaucracy. Although, his health and vision deteriorated in old age he remained mentally alert and interested in the AMH up to his death in 1994 at the age of 87.

Postscript

Atkinson Morley's gift to St. George's Hospital has stood in Copse Hill, Wimbledon for over one hundred and twenty five years. Although he left ample funds for its solid construction, its time as a convalescent hospital was dogged by jerry-building as a result of a penny pinching attitude, the responsibility for which has to be laid at the door of the tight-fisted Governors of St. George's Hospital who could appreciate the value of the facility, but were not prepared to pay for it. They wanted to save their money for more acute services, and probably felt that the hospital should be run on a low-cost budget as it was rather a luxury. This view tended to obscure the premise on which it had been built: to restore patients to normal health as quickly as possible, thus reducing the multiple costs, financial and otherwise, which were incurred in protracted ill-health. That others were going to reap the benefit tended to blinker the altruism of those that were providing the facility in the here and now. It is fair to say that despite niggling problems of this sort the great promise attached to it's foundation as the first of its kind, was fully borne out as expectation gradually turned into reality. Since the dramatic and sudden change of use in the 1940's its standing has risen with its development as a neuroscience centre for the treatment of patients with neurological and psychiatric disorders has been unparalleled. It has gained an international reputation which attracts visitors from all around the world. All are impressed by the quality of care and the teaching that it provides, but some are surprised that the appearance of the Atkinson Morley's is quite unlike a hospital and more akin to a nineteenth century French chateau. The story is told that one American visitor arriving by taxi, entered the entrance hall and asked the hall porter 'Where is the famous Atkinson Morley's Hospital?' The porter replied

'This is it, sir'. 'Gee' said the American 'I must have come through the back door!'

Despite the fact that the hospital was built on the cheap, and the fabric had to be restored on several occasions in the last century, it seems to have become structurally more sturdy with the passage of time. Routine maintenance is required which, of course, would be the case with any building, but there appears to have been no major work needed for many years, so perhaps it is just taking rather a long time to settle down to a solid and stable old age? This jerry-built old convalescent hospital now consists of a multitude of extensions and annexes which would render it unrecognisable to the original builders. Although its age and the *ad hoc* nature of some of the internal structures leaves much to be desired in aesthetic terms, it has one enormous advantage over many contemporary hospitals, and that is the fact that it is built on a human scale far removed from the soulless anonymity and bewildering uniformity enshrined in modern design. This, and the fact that it is small enough for all who work in it to know one another and their individual contributions to the whole makes it loved and appreciated by patients, relatives, visitors and staff. It exudes an atmosphere of warmth, helpful understanding and professionalism. It is unique.

Most of the staff and the patients are sad that the hospital is likely to close before the end of the century and its services will be transferred into a new block at St. George's Hospital, Tooting. The hospital has been under threats of this type frequently in the past, and a great deal of effort has been put into attempts to ward off predators, and those who would save us from ourselves. The name of Atkinson Morley should be preserved at all costs so that future generations of staff, students and patients may be made aware of the debt that St. George's, the Neurosciences, and the Community at Large owe to the benevolence of this self-effacing nineteenth century hotel owner.

Index